Using STEM Investigate Issues in Managing Waste

Authors: Barbara R. Sandall, Ed.D., and Abha Singh, Ph.D.
Consultants: Schrylet Cameron and Suzanne Myers
Editors and Proofreader: Mary Dieterich, Sarah M. Anderson, and Margaret Brown

COPYRIGHT © 2011 Mark Twain Media, Inc.

ISBN 978-1-58037-580-1

Printing No. CD-404143

Mark Twain Media, Inc., Publishers
Distributed by Carson-Dellosa Publishing LLC

Visit us at www.carsondellosa.com

Table of Contents

Introduction to *Using STEM to Investigate Issues in Managing Waste*

Introduction to the Series

The *STEMs of Learning: Science, Technology, Engineering, and Mathematics* is an initiative designed to get students interested in these career fields. In 2009, the National Academy of Engineering (NAE) and the National Research Council (NRC) reported that there is a lack of focus on the science, technology, engineering, and mathematics (STEM) subjects in K–12 schools. This creates concerns about the competitiveness of the United States in the global market and the development of a workforce with the knowledge and skills needed to address technical and technological issues. The focus of many current STEM education programs is on mathematics and science and not on engineering and technology. This series was developed to encourage students to become a part of the solution and increase interest in the STEM areas. The series introduces students to the use of STEM skills to solve problems. It is our hope that through these investigations students will become interested in the STEM areas of study.

The *Using STEM to Investigate Series* provides fun and meaningful integrated activities that cultivate an interest in topics in the STEM fields of science, technology, engineering, and mathematics and encourage students to explore careers in these fields. The series introduces students to the following topics: Issues in Alternative Energy, Issues in Food Production, and Issues in Managing Waste using science, mathematics, engineering, and technological design as a means for problem solving and scientific inquiry. Students actively engage in solving real-world problems using scientific inquiry, content knowledge, and technological design. All of the activities are aligned with the National Science Education (NSE) Standards, the National Council of Teachers of Mathematics (NCTM) Standards, and the International Technology Education Association (ITEA) Standards for Technological Literacy. For correlations to state, national, and Canadian provincial standards, visit www.carsondellosa.com.

The series is written for classroom teachers, parents, families, and students. The books in this series can be used as a full unit of study or as individual lessons to supplement existing curriculum programs or textbooks. Activities are designed to be pedagogically sound, hands-on, minds-on activities that support the national standards. Parents and students can use this series as an enhancement to what is done in the classroom or as a tutorial at home. The procedures and content background are clearly explained in the introduction and within the individual activities. Materials used are commonly found in classrooms and homes or can be ordered from science supply sources.

Science, Technology, and Society

Science, technology, and society are closely related. Science and technology impact personal and community health, population growth, natural resources, and environmental quality. It is important for students to understand the interrelationship of science, technology, and society because these factors

Introduction to *Using STEM to Investigate Issues in Managing Waste* (cont.)

impact their daily lives all over the world. Science advances new technology, and using new technology increases scientific knowledge.

Science and technology are pursued for different reasons. Science inquiry is driven by the desire to understand the natural world. Technology is driven by the need to solve problems and meet human needs. Technology usually has more of a direct effect on society. For example, the creation of the telephone, computers, and the Internet have had a large impact on the way our society communicates. Science and technology have also impacted the diagnoses and treatment of diseases that have increased the longevity of the human race. Science and technology have created more comfortable places for us to live in most areas of the world. However, science and technology have also had a negative impact on our environment. As a new technology that we need or want is developed, the impact on the environment must be closely examined.

The National Science Education Standards (NSES) unifying concepts and science processes skills integrate the areas of science, technology, engineering, and mathematics (STEM). The unifying concepts include systems, order, and organization; evidence, models, and explanations; change, constancy, and measurement; evolution and equilibrium; and form and function. The processes of inquiry are skills used in all content areas and in our everyday lives to investigate and solve problems. These science process skills include the basic skills of classifying, observing, measuring, inferring, communicating, predicting, manipulating materials, replicating, using numbers, developing vocabulary, questioning, and using cues. The integrated science process skills include creating models, formulating a hypothesis, generalizing, identifying and controlling variables, defining operationally, recording and interpreting data, making decisions, and experimenting. See the Appendix for a list of skills and definitions.

Technological Design Process

The NSES recommend that students have abilities and understandings of technological design and about science and technology. The NSES Science and Technology Content Standard E states that the technological design process includes identifying a problem or design opportunity; proposing designs and possible solutions; implementing the solution; evaluating the solution and its consequences; and communicating the problem, processes, and solution. Creativity, imagination, and a good content background are necessary in working in science and engineering. The process is a continuous cycle.

The International Technology Education Association (ITEA) Standards for Technological Literacy also suggest that students develop abilities for a technological world that include applying the design process to solve a problem, using and maintaining technological products, and assessing the impact of the products on the environment and society. Students should have an understanding of the attributes of design and engineering design and the role of troubleshooting, research and

Introduction to *Using STEM to Investigate Issues in Managing Waste* (cont.)

development, inventions and innovations, and experimentation in problem solving. The design process includes identifying and collecting information about everyday problems that can be solved by technology. It also includes generating ideas and requirements for solving the problems.

Mathematical Problem Solving

The National Council of Teachers of Mathematics (NCTM) recommend that students develop abilities to use problem-solving skills, formulate problems, develop and apply a variety of strategies to solve problems, verify and interpret results, and generalize solutions and strategies to new problems. Students also need to be able to communicate with models, orally, in writing, and with pictures and graphs; reflect and clarify their own thinking; use the skills of reading, listening, and observing to interpret and evaluate ideas; and be able to make conjectures and convincing arguments. Students should be able to recognize and apply reasoning processes, make and evaluate arguments, validate their own thinking, and use the power of reasoning to solve problems. All of these skills are related to science and technology, as well as mathematics.

Introduction to Waste Management

Environmental engineers try to solve problems related to air, water, and soil contamination. These contaminations may come from human activity or from the human use of technology. Humans need clean air, clean water, and good soil to live. One of the problems environmental engineers are trying to solve is how to safely dispose of waste products from homes, businesses, industry, and so on. Other problems are how to clean up water, air, and soil that is already contaminated.

In the past, garbage was just dumped into the streets. As early as 500 B.C., Athens, Greece, created a law prohibiting the dumping of garbage in the streets. They created the first municipal disposal site by requiring garbage to be dumped not less than a mile from Athens. Careless waste disposal created problems because piles of garbage multiplied as cities grew. This forced city governments to take on the collection and disposal of garbage. At this time, they took the garbage outside of town and dumped it in open dumps. As cities grew, land where garbage could be dumped was harder to find, the odors became worse, and rats invaded the dumps. Some cities created pits for garbage, but these contaminated the groundwater. In 1874, Nottingham, England, developed the first waste incinerator to burn garbage. The incineration took care of part of the problem, but it was costly and caused air pollution. In the 1900s, burying waste became the most common method of waste disposal.

The United States developed laws to protect human health and navigable waterways from pollution. The 1948 Water Pollution Control Act promoted research into the causes and solutions of water pollution. In the 1950s, there was an increase in solid waste because of new products and new packaging. This increase in solid waste created a need for trucks that compacted the garbage when it was collected. The federal Solid Waste Disposal Act, 1965, provided money to study solid waste disposal methods. This study revealed environmental problems and public health and safety issues resulting from landfills. From the 1970s to the present, more laws have been enacted to make landfills safer for people, animals, and the environment.

Introduction to *Using STEM to Investigate Issues in Managing Waste* (cont.)

Millions of people throw things into the trash every day. Some of that trash can become a valuable resource for new materials and new uses. There are five R's in examining the issues involved in waste management. **Reduce** the amount of waste you produce. **Reuse** the objects for new purposes. **Recycle** wastes into new materials. **Rethink** your values and your life style. **Re-buy** recycled products. People may have to examine their values and decide what they are willing to give up in order to help improve the quality of the environment. One of the purposes of this book on managing wastes is to help students make informed decisions that will help them reduce, reuse, recycle, and rethink the ways waste is managed.

There are four large categories for solid wastes: general waste, metal waste, paper waste, and plastic waste. General wastes include municipal solid waste, aseptic boxes, food wastes, glass containers, lead-acid batteries, scrap tires, and yard wastes. Aluminum packing and steel cars are some metal wastes. Paper wastes include corrugated boxes, magazines, newspapers, and office paper. There are also many kinds of plastic wastes including high-density polyethylene (HDPE), plastic film, and polyethylene terephthalate (PET).

The National Solid Waste Management Association (NSWMA) was founded in 1962 to promote the management of waste "in a manner that is environmentally responsible, efficient, profitable, and ethical, while benefiting the public and protecting employees." Greenhouse gases, electronic wastes, health care wastes, landfills, and transportation of wastes are some of the issues involved in handling solid wastes

Society depends on electronic products in a variety of forms. Televisions, radios, cell phones, computers, and so on are just some of the products available today. In 2006, the United States Government Accountability Office estimated that over 100 million computers, monitors, and televisions become obsolete each year. Many of these products are made with lead and other heavy metals. These metals leach into the environment when electronic waste is put into solid waste landfills. The U.S. Environmental Protection Agency estimates that electronic waste is the largest contributor to the heavy metals found in landfills. Managing electronic wastes has become a major issue in waste management. Hundreds of companies and organizations are now processing electronic wastes for reuse and recycling.

In this book, students will be investigating different kinds of wastes and waste disposal. The activities will introduce the issues that must be considered in getting rid of wastes. By using science inquiry and integrated activities, students will solve real-world problems and be encouraged to explore careers in the waste management fields. Each unit in this book provides content background information in waste management topics; hands-on activities that demonstrate how science, technology, engineering, and mathematics can be applied to problems in this field; and assessments that check students' mastery of the written material and the interactive projects.

Chapter One: Waste Management Issues

Teacher Information

Topic: Issues in waste management

Standards:
NSES – Unifying Concepts and Processes
Systems, Order, and Organization
Form and Function

NSES – Content
NSES A: Science as Inquiry
NSES B: Physical Science
NSES C: Life Science
NSES D: Earth and Space
NSES E: Science and Technology
NSES F: Personal and Social Perspectives
NSES G: Science as a Human Endeavor

NCTM:
Problem Solving
Communication
Reasoning
Mathematical Connections
Probability

ITEA:
Nature of Technology
Technology and Society
Technological World

Concepts:
Solid wastes
Waste management
Recycling, reducing, reusing materials
Getting rid of solid wastes
Impact of solid wastes on the environment
Making decisions about what to do with solid wastes
Pollution
Environmental impact of waste

Objectives:
Students will be able to…
- Examine their own beliefs and values to make decisions related to getting rid of solid wastes.
- Debate the issues, respecting the rights of others to maintain different rights and values.
- Evaluate possible solutions to waste management problems.
- Explain what needs to be considered when making decisions about managing solid wastes.

Activity – Waste Management Issue Discussion Sheets (p. 6–13)

Materials:
    Issue Discussion Sheets

TEACHER NOTE: The major purpose of this activity is to help students learn about the issues involved in waste management. Prior to starting, the teacher should discuss the rules for discussion (i.e., all students have the right to their own opinions, they will listen and respect each other's ideas, etc.) Reproduce the number of sets of sheets needed for groups of four students. Each group should have a set.

Chapter One: Waste Management Issues

Student Information

Topic: Issues in waste management

Concepts:
Solid wastes
Waste management
Recycling, reducing, reusing materials
Getting rid of solid wastes
Impact of solid wastes on the environment
Making decisions about what to do with solid wastes
Pollution
Environmental impact of waste

Objectives:
Students will be able to…
- Examine their own beliefs and values to make decisions related to getting rid of solid wastes.
- Debate the issues, respecting the rights of others to maintain different rights and values.
- Evaluate possible solutions to waste management problems.
- Explain what needs to be considered when making decisions about managing solid wastes.

Content Background:

In 2008, residents and businesses in the United States produced 250 million tons of municipal solid waste, or 4.5 pounds of waste per person per day. The Environmental Protection Agency (EPA) states that of the 250 million tons of waste, 31% is paper; 13.2% is yard wastes; 12.7% is food; 12% is plastic; 8.4 % is metal; 7.9% is rubber, leather, and textiles; 6.6% is wood; 4.9% is glass; and 3.3% is other materials.

There are four large categories for solid wastes: general waste, metal waste, paper waste, and plastic waste. General wastes include municipal solid waste, aseptic boxes, food wastes, glass containers, lead-acid batteries, scrap tires, and yard wastes. Aluminum packing and steel cars are some metal wastes. Paper wastes include corrugated boxes, magazines, newspapers, and office paper. There are also many kinds of plastic wastes including high-density polyethylene (HDPE), plastic film, and polyethylene terephthalate (PET).

Examples of municipal solid waste are product packaging, grass clippings, furniture, clothing, bottles, food, newspapers, appliances, paint, and batteries. When these items wear out or are replaced by something else, they become a part of the waste stream. A **waste stream** is the general flow of waste from the time it is thrown away until it is destroyed or buried.

Some items are actually designed to wear out or fail after a certain time. This is called **planned obsolescence**. An example of planned obsolescence is car tires that must be replaced after a certain number of miles.

Waste management practices include recycling, composting, source reduction, landfills, and incineration. The EPA ranks the most environmentally sound solutions for solid waste. The most preferred method is source reduction, then recycling and composting, and lastly, disposal by incineration and landfills. In the United States, 33.2% of

Chapter One: Waste Management Issues

Student Information

the waste is recovered and recycled or composted, 12.6% is incinerated, and 54% is put into landfills.

There are five R's in waste management. **Reduce** the amount of waste you produce. **Reuse** the objects for new purposes. **Recycle** wastes into new materials. **Rethink** your values and your lifestyle. **Re-buy** recycled products. People may have to examine their values and decide what they are willing to give up in order to help improve the quality of the environment.

Recycling turns materials that would be waste into resources. Recycling protects manufacturing jobs, reduces the need for landfills and incineration, prevents pollution caused by the manufacturing of new products, saves energy, decreases emissions of greenhouse gases, conserves natural resources, and helps sustain the environment. Recycling removes glass, plastic, paper, and metals from the waste stream. The recycled materials are processed and manufactured into new products, and then they are sold. There are three steps to recycling a product: collecting and processing, manufacturing, and purchasing recycled products.

Organic materials, such as yard trimmings, food scraps, wood waste, and paper, are the largest component of our solid wastes. They make up about two-thirds of the solid waste. Composting organic materials will help to reduce this waste. **Composting** decomposes **organic** (was once living or carbon based) waste using microorganisms—mainly bacteria and fungi—to break down the material into a usable form. The organic materials decompose to produce humus that can be used for fertilizer.

In the woods, gardens, and grass, natural composting happens when vegetation and animals die and fall to the ground. As this organic matter decays, it provides minerals and nutrients needed for plants, animals, and microorganisms. Some people are now composting their plant wastes to use as fertilizer on home gardens.

Source reduction is altering the design, manufacture, or use of products and materials to reduce the amount of toxicity of what is thrown away as waste. Grass-cycling or mulching grass clippings, backyard composting, copying on two sides of paper, and reducing transport packaging in industry are examples of source reduction.

Landfills are areas that have been created to store solid wastes. Sanitary landfills are engineered to protect the environment from contami-

Chapter One: Waste Management Issues

Student Information

nants. The landfill siting laws prevent placing landfills in environmentally sensitive areas and require environmental monitoring systems that monitor groundwater contamination. They also require safety systems to be in place.

Landfills also need to be monitored for greenhouse gases. Landfills release methane, nitrous oxide, and carbon dioxide. The total emissions are 2.25% of the U.S. greenhouse gas emissions. To alleviate this problem, waste-to-energy landfills collect methane gas emissions to convert the gas to energy for heat and electricity. Other landfill facilities use oxidation of the methane or burning of the collected gases.

Between 1974 and 1997, increased recycling, composting, waste-to-energy sites, and landfill gas reductions reduced the greenhouse gas emissions by 78%. Landfills store carbon due to incomplete degradation of organic materials as the material degrades slowly. Recycling and composting reduced greenhouse gases by 2.5% in 2005, and 85 million tons of municipal solid wastes were recycled or composted in 2007. This is a great improvement, but more needs to be done.

Another way to control solid waste is incineration. **Incineration** is a controlled high-temperature burning of solid waste materials. This process

helps reduce the amount of space needed for a landfill. Recyclable materials can be removed from the wastes before burning. The burning waste can be used to heat water to fuel heating systems or generate electricity.

Pollution controls must be built into the incineration process to control the gases given off during the burning process. Scrubbers and filters are added to the chimneys to remove the gases and ash particles given off. Burning waste at high temperatures destroys chemical compounds and disease-causing bacteria. Ash from the incineration process is monitored to be sure it is non-hazardous so it can be used for daily cover in landfills and road construction.

Commercial and industrial waste is a significant portion of municipal waste. Commercial and industrial waste are usually collected by private waste haulers, and recyclable materials are not always recovered. The EPA has guidelines that will help communities more effectively handle commercial and industrial waste and meet high waste recovery goals. These guidelines can be found at <http://www.epa.gov/epawaste/non-haz/industrial/index.htm>. Communities need to examine how to safely and effectively manage these wastes.

Non-municipal solid wastes include agricultural wastes. Runoff from agricultural land is also considered solid waste. Agricultural runoff includes herbicides, pesticides, and fertilizers. **Herbicides** are used to control weeds, and **pesticides** are used to

Chapter One: Waste Management Issues

Student Information

control or destroy pests, such as insects. **Fertilizers** are used to enrich the soil so the crops grow better. The environmental impact of the use of these chemicals needs to be studied and alternatives to using them need to be found.

Monitoring and controlling how waste is disposed of is also a health issue. In early European countries, wastes and waste products were just thrown in gutters in the streets. The Plague spread rapidly in these areas.

The World Health Organization (WHO) reports that garbage collection services are still very poor in developing nations. Thirty to fifty percent of wastes go uncollected in these nations. Some countries still have open sewers to transport human wastes, which can carry diseases. Most developing countries have open waste dump sites with waste pickers (people who go through the open garbage). The problem is that in the past 20 years, solid wastes in these countries have increased 50–100% with no way of collecting the waste materials.

Proper management of hazardous household waste is also an issue related to waste management. There are four categories of hazardous substances: corrosive, flammable, reactive, and toxic. **Corrosive** materials eat away materials by a chemical reaction. Oven cleaners, toilet bowl cleaners, and battery acid are corrosive materials. **Flammable** materials ignite easily. Lighter fluid, gasoline, paint remover, and varnish are flammable, or ignitable. **Reactive** materials create an explosion or produce deadly vapors when exposed to heat, air, water, shock, or when mixed with other chemicals. Bleach mixed with ammonia-based cleaners is reactive. **Toxic** materials are poisonous when eaten, touched, or inhaled, even in small amounts. Pesticides, cleaning fluids, bleach, and some metals like lead are toxic.

An average home contains numerous products with warning labels on them. Read all labels before disposing or storing materials. None of these materials should be placed in a landfill because they will leach into the ground and water and become hazards to the environment, animals, and people.

This chapter will introduce the issues involved in monitoring and controlling the waste stream.

Name: _____   Date: _____

Chapter One: Waste Management Issues

Student Activity

Activity – Issues in Managing Wastes

Materials:

> Issue Discussion Sheets

Challenge Question: Identify the best way to get rid of municipal solid waste.

Procedure:

1. Divide the class into groups and give each group a set of issue discussion sheets.
2. One person in the group takes an issue sheet, reads it to the group, and explains the decision they have chosen and why they have made that decision.
3. The other members of the group then share whether they agree or disagree and why they agree or disagree.
4. This continues until all of the issues are discussed in the small groups.

Challenges:

1. On your own paper, design an ideal waste management facility.

2. On your own paper, design a plan for waste management in your community.

Name: _____   Date: _____

Chapter One: | Waste Management Issues

Waste Management Issue Discussion Sheets

- -

Issue 1 – Landfills

Landfills are areas that have been created to store solid wastes. If landfills are engineered and constructed properly, they will protect the environment from contaminants. Landfills handle large amounts of solid waste materials. Municipal wastes (wastes from cities) are put into these landfills. Examples of municipal solid wastes are product packaging, grass clippings, furniture, clothing, bottles, food, newspapers, appliances, paint, and batteries.

Some materials are banned from landfills. Common household items that are banned include paints, cleaners, chemicals, motor oil, batteries, and pesticides. These products are considered hazardous wastes. If they are mishandled, they can be hazardous to human health and the environment. Some landfills have a hazardous waste drop-off station for these items.

Landfills release greenhouse gases, such as methane, nitrous oxide, and carbon dioxide. Greenhouse gases are suspected of contributing to global warming.

Not all landfills are the same. Some landfills use waste-to-energy procedures to collect methane gas emissions to convert the gas to energy for heat and electricity. Other landfill facilities use oxidation of the methane or burn the collected gases.

Question:

What should be done?

a. Build more landfill sites to accommodate all of the wastes we produce and do not regulate what kind is built.

b. All landfill facilities should be waste-to-energy, have household hazardous waste drop-off stations, recycle all materials that are recyclable, and remove all hazardous materials.

c. The government should mandate that all landfill facilities be waste-to-energy, have household hazardous waste drop-off stations, and recycle everything that can be recycled.

d. Everyone should work on source reduction.

e. Do something else. Explain.

Name: _____   Date: _____

Chapter One: Waste Management Issues

Waste Management Issue Discussion Sheets

Issue 2 – Electronic Wastes

In 2006, the United States Government Accountability Office (GAO) estimated that over 100 million computers, monitors, and televisions become obsolete each year. The U.S. Environmental Protection Agency (EPA) estimates that electronic waste is the largest contributor of heavy metals found in landfills. Managing electronic wastes has become a major issue in waste management. Hundreds of companies and organizations are now processing electronic wastes for reuse and recycling. However, there is no national strategy to recycle electronic wastes.

Question: What should be done?

a. Government financial incentives, such as tax credits to consumers, manufacturers, retailers, and recyclers, should be offered.

b. Require electronic device manufacturers to take trade-ins on new electronics purchased.

c. The federal government should require and fund electronic recycling programs in every community.

d. Everyone should reduce the amount of electronic technology currently being used.

e. Do something else. Explain.

8

Name: _____   Date: _____

Chapter One: Waste Management Issues

Waste Management Issue Discussion Sheets

- -

Issue 3 – Incineration

Incineration is a controlled high-temperature burning of solid waste materials. This process helps reduce the amount of space needed for a landfill, kills harmful bacteria and other organisms, can produce energy for heat systems, and can generate electricity.

The high temperatures of incineration kill disease-causing bacteria and change the chemical makeup of the wastes. This is especially important with medical wastes that can be incinerated to kill bacteria, germs, viruses, etc.

Incineration can generate energy while reducing the amount of waste 90% in volume and 75% in weight.

During incineration, the gases emitted into the air must be closely monitored. Emissions are sent through scrubbers that use a liquid spray to neutralize the acid gases and filters that remove tiny ash particles.

Question: What should be done?

a. Build more incineration plants as fast as they can be built, and do not worry about the government mandates as to how they are built.

b. Build more incineration plants, making sure they remove all recyclable materials prior to burning and that they are equipped with scrubbers, filters, and other equipment to ensure that the incinerators are safe to operate and do not pollute the environment.

c. Discontinue the use of incinerators because they can cause pollution and excess heat.

d. Build more incineration plants to burn all solid wastes, making sure that they are equipped with scrubbers, filters, and other equipment to ensure that the incinerators are safe to operate and do not pollute the environment.

e. Do something else. Explain.

Name: _____ Date: _____

Chapter One: Waste Management Issues

Waste Management Issue Discussion Sheets

- -

Issue 4 – Composting

Composting decomposes organic waste using microorganisms—mainly bacteria and fungi—to break down the materials. When the decomposition process is done, the material left is a nutrient-rich substance that looks like soil and can be added to gardens, flower beds, fields, and other areas where planting is done.

Things that can be composted are animal manure (excluding pet wastes), cardboard rolls, clean paper, coffee grounds and filters, cotton rags, dryer and vacuum cleaner lint, eggshells, fireplace ash, fruits and vegetables, yard clippings, hair and fur, hay, straw, houseplants, leaves, nut shells, sawdust, shredded newspaper, tea bags, and wool rags. Some things that should not be composted are black walnut leaves and twigs, coal or charcoal ash, dairy products, fats, grease, lard, oils, meat or fish scraps, pet wastes, or yard trimmings that have been chemically treated.

According to the EPA, compost can suppress plant disease and pests; reduce or eliminate the need for chemical fertilizers; provide higher yields; facilitate reforestation, wetlands restoration, and habitat revitalization; cost-effectively remediate contaminated soils; remove solids, grease, and heavy metals from storm water runoff; capture and destroy 99.6% of industrial volatile organic chemicals in contaminated air; and provide cost savings over other remediation technologies.

Question: What should be done?

a. Everyone should save the environment and start their own compost pile in their backyard immediately.

b. Everyone should be encouraged to compost their food and yard wastes in their backyard.

c. The government should pay everyone to compost all of their yard wastes and the plant materials left over from eating fruits and vegetables.

d. City governments should offer curbside pick-up of compostable materials and operate a city compost site.

e. Do something else. Explain.

 10

Name: _____   Date: _____

Chapter One: | Waste Management Issues

Waste Management Issue Discussion Sheets

- -

Issue 5 – Commercial and Industrial Waste Management

In the United States, industrial facilities generate 7.6 billion tons of solid waste per year. Commercial and industrial waste is a significant portion of municipal waste. Commercial and industrial waste is usually collected by private waste haulers, and recyclable materials are not always recovered.

The EPA has guidelines that will help communities more effectively handle commercial and industrial waste and meet high waste recovery goals. Recommendations are to understand the risks of commercial and industrial wastes; identify the wastes being produced and how pollution can be prevented; consider where to dump the wastes; and identify the impact of the waste site on air, surface water, and groundwater quality. Communities should also consider the long-term management of the waste: operating the waste management system, monitoring the performance of the system, taking corrective actions as needed, and having a plan for closure of the system when it is full or no longer needed.

Question: What should be done?

a. Allow commercial and industrial waste haulers to dump materials wherever they want.

b. Encourage community leaders to work with commercial and industrial waste producers in the area to determine what wastes are being dumped into landfills and how the materials should be handled.

c. The government should mandate that community leaders work with commercial and industrial waste producers in the area to determine what wastes are being dumped into landfills and how the materials should be handled.

d. Everyone in the community should work together with the community leaders, the EPA, government officials, and commercial and industrial waste producers to identify the wastes in the area and determine the best solution to manage the wastes.

e. Do something else. Explain.

Name: _____   Date: _____

Chapter One: Waste Management Issues

Waste Management Issue Discussion Sheets

- -

Issue 6 – Recycling, Reusing, Reducing, Rethinking Values and Life Styles, and Re-buying Recycled Materials

In 2008, residents and businesses in the United States produced 250 million tons of municipal solid waste or 4.5 pounds of waste per person per day. One way to reduce solid wastes in landfills is through source reduction. Source reduction or waste prevention is accomplished by reducing the amount of waste you produce. Source reduction strategies include grass-cycling, composting, two-sided copying, and transport packaging reduction. Reusing objects for new purposes and recycling wastes into new materials can keep waste out of landfills. By rethinking your values and your lifestyle, you can come up with ways to reduce the waste you produce. You can also re-buy items made from recycled materials, which creates a demand for recycled items. This makes it profitable for companies to manufacture goods using recycled materials.

Questions: What can be done to prevent wastes?

a. Purchase items that have the least amount of packaging.

b. Only purchase what is needed, not what is wanted. Do not buy something just because it is the latest technology or newest thing. In other words, use what you have until it wears out.

c. Separate your trash into recyclable and non-recyclable items.

d. Buy recycled materials when they are available.

e. All of the above.

Name: _____ Date: _____

Chapter One: Waste Management Issues

Waste Management Issue Discussion Sheets

- -

Issue 7 – Hazardous Household Waste

There are four categories of hazardous substances: corrosive, flammable, reactive, and toxic. Corrosive substances eat away materials by a chemical reaction. Oven cleaners, toilet bowl cleaners, and battery acid are corrosive substances. Flammable materials ignite easily. Lighter fluid, gasoline, paint remover, and varnish are flammable, or ignitable. Reactive materials create an explosion or produce deadly vapors when exposed to heat, air, water, or shock, or when mixed with other chemicals. For example, bleach mixed with ammonia-based cleaners is a reactive material. Toxic substances are poisonous when eaten, touched, or inhaled, even in small amounts. Pesticides, cleaning fluids, bleach, and some metals like lead are toxic.

An average home contains numerous products with warning labels on them. Read all labels before disposing of or storing materials that may be hazardous. The labels should give you guidelines on how to safely store and dispose of these materials. If you place these items in your household trash or recycling bin, they could harm you, the sanitation workers who pick up your trash or handle it at the landfill, animals that might get into your trash, or the environment if the materials spill at some point.

Question: So what do you do with these materials?

a. Throw hazardous wastes in the trash when you are finished with them.

b. Throw them in the recycle bin when you are finished.

c. Read the labels and dispose of the hazardous materials as the label recommends.

d. Take the materials to a hazardous waste recycling center.

e. Do something else. Explain.

Chapter One: Waste Management Issues

Investigate Further: Waste Management Issues

Websites

Alternative Energy News: Waste Energy
   http://www.alternative-energy-news.info/
   technology/garbage-energy/

The Daily Green: What do Recycling Symbols on Plastics Mean?
   http://www.thedailygreen.com/green-homes/
   latest/recycling-symbols-plastics-460321

Energy Recovery Council: Waste to Energy
   http://www.wte.org

Environmental Protection Agency (EPA)
   www.epa.gov/

   Guide for Industrial Waste Management
     http://www.epa.gov/epawaste/nonhaz/
     industrial/guide/index.htm

   Inventory of Greenhouse Gas Emissions and Sinks: 1990 – 2008
     http://www.epa.gov/climatechange/
     emissions/usinventoryreport.html

   Landfill Methane Outreach Program
     http://www.epa.gov/lmop/index.html

   Non-Hazardous Wastes
     http://www.epa.gov/epawaste/basic-solid.
     htm

   Planet Protectors Club for Kids
     http://www.epa.gov/epawaste/education/
     kids/planetprotectors/index.htm

   Reducing and Recycling
     http://www.epa.gov/epawaste/conserve/
     materials/organics/reduce.htm

   Solid Waste Management and Greenhouse Gases: A Life-Cycle Assessment of Emissions and Sinks
     http://epa.gov/climatechange/wycd/waste/
     downloads/fullreport.pdf

   Waste Reduction Through Conservation
     http://www.epa.gov/epawaste/conserve/
     rrr/reduce.htm

   Wastes
     www.epa.gov/epawaste/

National Center for Technological Literacy: Museum of Science, Boston
   http://www.nctl.org/

   Our Nation's Challenge
     http://www.nctl.org/our_nations_
     challenge.php

Recology: Residential Compost Collection Program
   http://sunsetscavenger.com/
   residentialCompost.htm

World Health Organization: Waste Management
   http://www.wpro.who.int/health_topics/
   waste_management/

Books

Winter, Jonah. *Here Comes the Garbage Barge!* New York: Schwartz & Wade. 2010.

Name: _____   Date: _____

Chapter One: Waste Management Issues

Waste Management Issues Assessment

Objectives:

Students will be able to…

- Examine their own beliefs and values related to getting rid of solid wastes.
- Debate the issues, respecting the rights of others to maintain different rights and values.
- Evaluate possible solutions to the waste management problem.
- Explain what needs to be considered when making decisions about managing solid wastes.

Matching:

_____ 1. Commercial and industrial waste

_____ 2. Non-municipal wastes

_____ 3. Incineration

_____ 4. Landfill

_____ 5. Electronic waste

_____ 6. Composting

_____ 7. Reduce

_____ 8. Reuse

_____ 9. Recycle

_____ 10. Re-buy

_____ 11. Rethink

_____ 12. Source reduction

a. Usually collected by private waste haulers and recyclables are not always recovered.

b. Agricultural wastes including runoff from herbicides, pesticides, and fertilizers

c. Area created to store solid wastes

d. Altering the design, manufacture, or use of products to reduce the toxicity of what is thrown away

e. Decomposing organic materials using microorganisms to break it down into a usable form

f. High-temperature burning of wastes

g. Discarded computers, radios, cell phones, television monitors, etc.

h. Cut back on the amount of waste produced

i. Use objects for new purposes

j. Make wastes into new products

k. Examine your values and make changes to improve the environment

l. Purchase recycled materials

Name: _____   Date: _____

13. Describe the job of an environmental engineer.

_____

_____

_____

_____

_____

_____

_____

_____

_____

14. Explain what would happen if we did not have landfills, incinerators, and other ways of disposing of wastes.

_____

_____

_____

_____

_____

_____

_____

_____

Chapter Two: Solid Waste

Teacher Information

Topic: Solid Waste

Standards:

NSES – Unifying Concepts and Processes
Systems, Order, and Organization
Form and Function

NSES – Content
NSES A: Science as Inquiry
NSES B: Physical Science
NSES C: Life Science
NSES D: Earth and Space
NSES E: Science and Technology
NSES F: Personal and Social Perspectives
NSES G: Science as a Human Endeavor

NCTM:
Problem Solving
Communication
Reasoning
Mathematical Connections
Probability

ITEA:
Nature of Technology
Technology and Society
Technological World

Concepts:
Solid wastes
Sorting wastes by properties
Problems with waste disposal

Objectives:
Students will be able to…
- Place trash into categories.
- Identify recyclable wastes.
- Explain what is in the trash we throw out.
- Figure what the percentage one category of trash is of the whole.
- Describe how much of the waste thrown away could be recycled.

Activity: Sorting and Classifying Wastes (p. 20–23)

Materials: (for each group)
TEACHER PREPARATION – You may create your own average garbage bag for each group or use the following recipe:

100 cubic centimeters (cc) of average garbage
       37.5% (37.5 cc) paper and cardboard
       17.9% (17.9 cc) yard wastes (leaves, grass)
       6.7% (6.7 cc) glass – (marbles and bottles)
       8.3% (8.3 cc) plastic (plastic pieces)
       8.3% (8.3 cc) metal (foil, aluminum cans, steel cans, wire)
       6.7% (6.7 cc) food wastes – apple, carrots, bread, banana peels, celery, lettuce, etc. (no meat products)
       14.6% (14.6 cc) miscellaneous waste – wood, rubber, leather, etc.

Rubber gloves   Tongs
Newspapers   Marker
Box/container that is at least 10 x 10 x 10 cubic centimeters
Metric ruler

Chapter Two: Solid Waste

Student Information

Topic: Solid Waste

Concepts:
Solid wastes
Sorting wastes by properties
Problems with waste disposal

Objectives:
Students will be able to...
- Place trash into categories.
- Identify recyclable wastes.
- Explain what is in the trash we throw out.
- Figure what the percentage one category of trash is of the whole.
- Describe how much of the waste thrown away could be recycled.

Content Background:

In 2008, residents and businesses in the United States produced 250 million tons of municipal solid waste or 4.5 pounds of waste per person per day. The Environmental Protection Agency (EPA) states that of the 250 million tons of waste produced each year, 31% is paper; 13.2% yard wastes; 12.7% food; 12% plastic; 8.4 % metal; 7.9% rubber, leather, and textiles; 6.6% wood; 4.9% glass; and 3.3% other materials. Examples of mu-

nicipal solid waste are product packaging, grass clippings, furniture, clothing, bottles, food, newspapers, appliances, paint, and batteries.

It is important to learn about solid wastes because they are connected to resource and energy use, global warming, air pollution, water pollution, and so on. When these items wear out or are replaced by something else, they become a part of the waste stream. A **waste stream** is the general flow of waste from the time it is thrown away until it is destroyed or buried.

Some items are designed to wear out or fail after a certain time. This is called **planned obsolescence**. An example of planned obsolescence is car tires that must be replaced after a certain number of miles.

Waste management practices include recycling, reducing, reusing, composting, source reduction, landfills, and incineration. The EPA ranks the most environmentally sound solutions for solid waste. The most preferred method is source reduction, then recycling and composting, and lastly, disposal by incineration and landfills. In the United States, 33.2% of the waste is recovered and recycled or composted, 12.6% is incinerated, and 54% is put into landfills.

Organic materials such as yard trimmings, food scraps, wood waste, and paper are the larg-

Chapter Two: Solid Waste

Student Information

est component of our solid wastes. These make up about two-thirds of the solid waste. These materials can be easily composted into nutrients and minerals for plants. **Composting** is the decomposition of organic materials by microorganisms.

Incineration is a controlled high-temperature burning of solid waste materials. This process helps reduce the amount of space needed for a landfill. Recyclable materials can be removed from the wastes before burning. The burning waste can

be used to heat water to fuel heating systems or generate electricity. However, pollution controls must be built into the incineration process to control the gases given off during the burning process. Scrubbers and filters are added to the chimneys to remove the gases and ash particles given off.

Burning waste at high temperatures destroys chemical compounds and disease-causing bacteria. Incineration is frequently used to dispose of medical waste, since it takes care of the disease-causing bacteria and other infectious organisms. Ash is monitored to be sure it is non-hazardous so it can be used for daily cover in landfills and road construction.

Source reduction is altering the design, manufacture, or use of products and materials to reduce the amount of toxicity of what is thrown away as waste. Source reduction also helps reduce the amount of solid wastes in landfills.

Commercial and industrial waste is a significant portion of municipal waste. Commercial and industrial waste is usually collected by private waste haulers. Private waste haulers do not always recover recyclable materials. Commercial and industrial facilities need to be aware of what happens to the solid wastes when it leaves their sites.

Non-municipal solid waste includes agricultural wastes. Runoff from agricultural land is considered a solid waste. Agricultural runoff includes herbicides, pesticides, and fertilizers.

This chapter will examine what types of solid wastes may go into landfills.

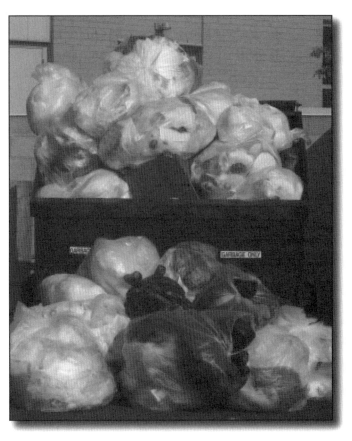

Name: _____   Date: _____

Chapter Two: Solid Waste

Student Activity

Activity: Sorting and Classifying Wastes

Materials:

100 cubic centimeters (cc) of average garbage (provided by the teacher)
     37.5% (37.5 cc) paper and cardboard
     17.9% (17.9 cc) yard wastes (leaves, grass)
     6.7% (6.7 cc) glass – (marbles and bottles)
     8.3% (8.3 cc) plastic (plastic pieces)
     8.3% (8.3 cc) metal (foil, aluminum cans, steel cans, wire)
     6.7% (6.7 cc) food wastes – apple, carrots, bread, banana peels,
      celery, lettuce, etc. (no meat products)
     14.6% (14.6 cc) miscellaneous waste – wood, rubber, leather, etc.

Rubber gloves   Tongs   Newspapers
Box / container that is at least 10 x 10 x 10 cubic centimeters
Marker   Metric ruler

Procedure:
1. Spread out newspapers on the table.
2. Pour out the sample bag of garbage.
3. Categorize the waste in the bag.
4. Record how you categorized the materials and what items were found in each category.

Results:

Type of Waste	Items

Name: _____　　Date: _____

Chapter Two: Solid Waste

Student Activity

1.　What properties did you use to separate the trash? _____

_____

_____

_____

_____

2.　What percentage of each item is in your trash? _____

_____

_____

3.　How could you find out? _____

_____

_____

One way of finding the percentage of each type of garbage is to measure the volume of each type.

　a.　Mark the inside of the box so the number of centimeters (height, depth, and width) can be measured.

　b.　Measure the amount of each item.

　c.　Record the amount in the data table

Category	Number of Cubic Centimeters (cc)	Percent of Total Amount of Garbage Number of cc of one type of garbage ÷ number of cc of total garbage

4.　Which category had the most? The least? _____

_____

Name: _____ Date: _____

Chapter Two: Solid Waste

Student Activity

5. Examine the table below showing the national average of garbage.

Type of Solid Waste	Percent of Total Amount of Garbage
Paper and cardboard	37.5%
Yard Wastes	17.9%
Miscellaneous – wood, rubber, leather, etc	14.6%
Plastic	8.3%
Metal	8.3%
Glass	6.7%
Food	6.7%

National Average – Center for Mathematics, Science, and Technology (1999) *Integrated Mathematics, Science, and Technology: Waste Management.* Peoria, IL: Glencoe

6. How does your data compare to the national averages of garbage?

_____

_____

_____

_____

_____

Conclusion:

1. What are solid wastes?

_____

_____

_____

_____

_____

_____

_____

Name: _____ Date: _____

Chapter Two: Solid Waste

Student Activity

2. Explain what would happen if we did not plan what to do with our solid wastes.

_____

_____

_____

_____

_____

_____

_____

_____

_____

3. What is the impact of solid wastes on the environment?

_____

_____

_____

_____

_____

_____

_____

_____

_____

Challenge:

On your own paper, design a plan to reduce solid waste going into landfills in your community.

Chapter Two: Solid Waste

Investigate Further: Municipal Solid Waste

The Daily Green: What do Recycling Symbols on Plastics Mean?

http://www.thedailygreen.com/green-homes/latest/recycling-symbols-plastics-460321

Department of Ecology: State of Washington: A Way with Waste Resources

http://www.ecy.wa.gov/programs/air/aawwaste/awwresources.html

Energy Recovery Council

http://www.wte.org

Environmental Protection Agency (EPA)

www.epa.gov/

Guide for Industrial Waste Management

http://www.epa.gov/epawaste/nonhaz/industrial/guide/index.htm

Inventory of Greenhouse Gas Emissions and Sinks: 1990 – 2008

http://www.epa.gov/climatechange/emissions/usinventoryreport.html

Landfill Methane Outreach Program

http://www.epa.gov/lmop/index.html

Non-Hazardous Wastes

http://www.epa.gov/epawaste/basic-solid.htm

Planet Protectors Club for Kids

http://www.epa.gov/epawaste/education/kids/planetprotectors/index.htm

The Quest for Less

http://www.epa.gov/wastes/education/quest/pdfs/qfl_complete.pdf

Reducing and Recycling

http://www.epa.gov/epawaste/conserve/materials/organics/reduce.htm

Solid Waste Management and Greenhouse Gases: A Life-Cycle Assessment of Emissions and Sinks

http://epa.gov/climatechange/wycd/waste/downloads/fullreport.pdf

Waste Reduction Through Conservation

http://www.epa.gov/epawaste/conserve/rrr/reduce.htm

Wastes

www.epa.gov/epawaste/

National Center for Technological Literacy: Museum of Science, Boston

http://www.nctl.org/

Our Nation's Challenge

http://www.nctl.org/our_nations_challenge.php

National Solid Waste Management Association (NSWMA)

http://www.environmentalistseveryday.org/

Electronic Wastes

http://www.environmentalistseveryday.org/issues-solid-waste-technologies-regulations/e-waste-disposal-electronics-products-computer-recycling/index.php

History of Solid Waste Management

http://www.environmentalistseveryday.org/publications-solid-waste-industry-research/information/history-of-solid-waste-managment/index.php

Recycling

http://www.environmentalistseveryday.org/issues-solid-waste-technologies-regulations/recycling-waste/index.php

Source Reduction

http://www.environmentalistseveryday.org/issues-solid-waste-technologies-regulations/source-reduction-solid-waste/index.php

Books

Winter, Jonah. *Here Comes the Garbage Barge!* New York: Schwartz & Wade. 2010.

Name: _____   Date: _____

Chapter Two: Solid Waste

Solid Waste Assessment

Objectives:

Students will be able to…

- Place trash into categories.
- Identify recyclable wastes.
- Explain what is in the trash we throw out.
- Figure what the percentage one category of trash is of the whole.
- Describe how much of the waste thrown away could be recycled.

Matching:

_____ 1. Incineration

_____ 2. Landfill

_____ 3. Municipal solid waste

_____ 4. Composting

_____ 5. Reduce, reuse, recycle

_____ 6. Planned obsolescence

_____ 7. Commercial and industrial waste

_____ 8. Source reduction

_____ 9. Waste stream

a. Area created to store solid wastes

b. Altering the design, manufacture, or use of products to reduce the toxicity of what is thrown away

c. Decomposing organic materials using microorganisms to break it down into a usable form

d. High-temperature burning of wastes

e. Waste from households and businesses in cities such as product packaging, grass clippings, furniture, food, and newspapers

f. Cut back on the amount of waste produced, use objects for new purposes, make wastes into new products

g. The general flow of waste from the time it is thrown away until it is destroyed or buried

h. Designing items to wear out or fail after a certain amount of time

i. Waste from businesses and industries, usually collected by private waste haulers

Name: _____ Date: _____

10. Explain why the recyclable materials in commercial and industrial waste may not be taken out before the waste is taken to a landfill.

_____

_____

_____

_____

11. Explain the advantages and disadvantages of incineration.

_____

_____

_____

_____

12. Explain the advantages and disadvantages of composting.

_____

_____

_____

_____

13. Describe the kinds of materials that go into a landfill.

_____

_____

_____

_____

14. Explain the difference between recyclable and non-recyclable materials.

_____

_____

_____

_____

Chapter Three: Product Life Cycle

Teacher Information

Topic: Life cycle of paper

Standards:
NSES – Unifying Concepts and Processes
Systems, Order, and Organization
Form and Function

NSES – Content
NSES A: Science as Inquiry
NSES B: Physical Science
NSES C: Life Science
NSES D: Earth and Space
NSES E: Science and Technology
NSES F: Personal and Social Perspectives
NSES G: Science as a Human Endeavor

NCTM:
Problem Solving
Communication
Reasoning
Mathematical Connections
Probability

ITEA:
Nature of Technology
Technology and Society
Technological World

Concepts:
Product life cycles
Environmental impact of products
Energy use

Objectives:
Students will be able to…
• Describe the life cycle of paper.
• Explain how energy is used in each stage of the life cycle of paper.
• Describe the resources needed to make paper.
• Explain the environmental impact of making paper.

• Conduct a life cycle assessment.
• Explain how paper can be recycled.

Activity 1: Life Cycle of Paper (p. 31)
Materials:
   Chart Paper   Markers

Activity 2: How Much Paper? (p. 32–33)
Materials:
   Paper   Pencils

Activity 3: Making Paper (p. 34–39)
Materials:
Paper – newspapers, paper towels, construction
   paper, tissue paper torn into small pieces

NOTE: Other papers may also be used – computer paper, magazines, egg cartons, paper bags, toilet paper, nonwaxed boxes, napkins, etc. If heavier paper is used, you may need to make the slurry in a blender. Dryer lint may also be used. Biodegradable packing peanuts could also be added. Newspaper will turn the new paper gray because of the ink in the paper.

Newspapers   Apron or smock
Warm water
Wooden frame - old picture frames can be used
Wire or nylon screen wire to fit the frame
Staples or tacks Paper towels
Spoon to stir the mixture
Disposable aluminum pan or plastic tub that the
   frame fits inside
2 Kitchen towels
Liquid Starch – optional to make the paper firmer
Glitter - optional
Dried flowers – optional
Rolling Pin - optional

TEACHER NOTE: This activity is messy.

Chapter Three: Product Life Cycle

Student Information

Topic: Life cycle of paper

Concepts:
Product life cycles
Environmental impact of products
Energy use

Objectives:
Students will be able to…
- Describe the life cycle of paper.
- Explain how energy is used in each stage of the life cycle of paper.
- Describe the resources needed to make paper.
- Explain the environmental impact of making paper.
- Conduct a life cycle assessment.
- Explain how paper can be recycled.

Content Background:

Written communication has been key throughout civilization. Early people drew on walls in caves to communicate. Later, the Sumerians wrote on clay tablets.

The word *paper* is derived from the Egyptian word *papyrus*. Papyrus is a plant that was found in Egypt about 5,000 years ago. Egyptians harvested and peeled and sliced the leaves into strips. The strips were layered and pounded together to make a flat uniform sheet on which they could write.

papyrus

Three thousand years later, Ts'ai Lun is credited with inventing paper in circa A.D. 104. He took the inner bark of a mulberry tree and bamboo fibers and mixed them with water. He pounded them and poured them on a coarsely woven cloth. Once it was dry, it formed a lightweight, easy to make, and relatively smooth writing surface.

In the 10th century, Arabians used wood and bamboo to make a higher-quality paper. Paper used today is made from trees, sawdust, saw mill scraps, and recycled paper. Currently paper is used in numerous ways, such as in notebooks, wrapping paper, wrapping items in a store, calendars, writing paper, cards, etc.

The life cycle of a product depends on what the product is, how it is made, and how it is used. Engineers conduct life-cycle assessments to try to solve problems and develop new technology. A **life-cycle assessment** examines all of the resources needed to create a product and the environmental impact of the product from its creation, through its use, up to its disposal. The environmental impact is the effect on the environment caused by humans or the technology that humans use.

A new product or technology is engineered to solve a problem or satisfy a need. The need or problem is identified, possible solutions to the problem are identified, and the product is created and tested. The product may undergo improvements, and then it is tested again, and eventually, it is sold to consumers. Throughout the

Chapter Three: Product Life Cycle

Student Information

development, distribution, use, and disposal of the new technology or product, resources and energy are required, and there may be an impact on the environment.

Resources are materials that are used to make a product or complete a task. **Energy** is the ability to do work. Energy may come from fuels to power machines for transportation or production of new materials. Energy also may be needed to develop new technology to make new products or technology.

The **life cycle of paper** begins when a tree is cut down. Cutting down a tree requires a saw, some type of energy to power the saw, and some type of energy to pick up the pieces of the tree and load the pieces onto some type of transportation that takes the wood to the paper mill. Energy and resources are needed to transport the wood to the paper mill and unload it.

When the tree arrives at the mill, the logs are chipped or ground into smaller pieces. Machines are needed to chop the wood into smaller pieces and some type of energy and resources are needed to run the machines. The chipped wood is heated with water and other chemicals until the wood is soft and mushy. At this stage it is called **pulp**. Some energy and resources are needed to get the water, heat the water, make the chemicals needed to soften the wood, and make the containers that contain the pulp.

The pulp is then put through machines with rollers to press the pulp into sheets. These roller machines require energy and resources to operate. Once the paper is made into sheets, it is allowed to dry. Once it is dry, the sheets are cut into smaller sheets, packaged, and transported to stores where the paper will be sold, which also takes energy and resources.

Consumers buy paper for business or home use and transport the paper to where it will be used. Energy and resources are used when the consumer buys, transports, and uses paper.

Paper is then discarded. Waste haulers pick up the discarded paper and recycle or put it into a landfill, which takes energy and resources. If the paper is recycled, the paper is sent back to a recycling facility where it is shredded and combined with water and other chemicals to create new pulp. The paper-making process starts over again. Recycling paper also takes energy and resources.

Some of the resources being used in making, using, and disposing of paper are trees; machines in the factories, cutting the tree, and transportation; chemicals to break down the wood and paper; water and some source of energy to heat the water; land for landfills; and machines and ma-

Chapter Three: Product Life Cycle

Student Information

terials for constructing the landfills or paper recycling facilities.

Conducting a life-cycle assessment of a product means the environmental impact throughout the whole cycle needs to be evaluated. Some of the environmental impacts from making paper are the loss of habitat, erosion, and more carbon dioxide in the atmosphere when the trees are cut. Trees provide habitat for animals that live in the trees and use the trees for food and shelter.

Erosion, the wearing away of soil from wind and water, occurs more after the trees in an area are cut. When the trees are not there to hold the soil in place, the soil wears away faster, carrying away all of the nutrients with it. Trees take in water and carbon dioxide from the air during the process of photosynthesis to make glucose and oxygen. Fewer trees means there is less carbon dioxide being taken out of the air and less oxygen being produced.

Many paper companies address this issue by managing private forests. In managed forests, one tree is planted for every tree that is cut. This way, the total number of trees in a forest remains constant.

Chemicals used in the paper-making process may be harmful to the environment, either while being used in the paper-making process, in the manufacturing of the chemicals, or the disposal of the chemicals. Air pollution may come from the paper-making factories or from transportation throughout the process. Disposal of the used paper may also cause pollution. If the used paper is dumped into a landfill, it could pollute the ground. If it is incinerated, unless the incinerator is built correctly, the smoke from the incinerator could pollute the air. Recycling facilities may also cause air pollution from transportation and remaking the paper.

Commercial paper mills have specific guidelines for construction of smokestacks so that the smokestacks do not pollute the air and only steam is given off. Many mills use recycled paper waste and wood waste to generate their own electricity. Wastewater can cause pollution problems, but in the United States and Canada, these are closely monitored. The pulp-cooking process can also cause odors, but mills have systems in place to reduce the amount of odor. At least half of commercial paper is made from lumber mill residues and from paper that is recycled, reducing the need to cut more trees.

Producing recycled paper requires 40% less energy, 70% less water pollution, and less air pollution than producing nonrecycled paper. In 2006, the United States recycled more than 50% of the paper it used, taking 50 million tons of paper out of the waste stream.

This chapter investigates the life cycle of paper and using recycled paper to make paper.

Name: _____ Date: _____

Chapter Three: Product Life Cycle

Student Activity

Activity 1: Life Cycle of Paper

Materials:

    Chart Paper   Markers

Challenge Question: Explain the life cycle of paper, starting with cutting the tree.

Procedure:

1. What is a life cycle assessment?

_____

_____

_____

_____

2. Create a model, diagram, or chart of the life cycle assessment of paper.
3. Label each step.
4. Describe the kinds of resources needed in each step.
5. Label where energy is needed in each step and what kind of energy is needed.
6. Use this space to explain what kinds of energy are needed in each step of your model.

_____

_____

_____

_____

_____

_____

7. Share your model with the class.
8. Once everyone has shared their models, compare all of the models. Do they represent a thorough life cycle assessment? Why or why not?

_____

_____

_____

_____

Name: _____   Date: _____

Chapter Three: Product Life Cycle

Student Activity

Activity 2: How Much Paper?

Materials:
Paper   Pencils

Challenge Question: How much paper is used in a classroom in a day?

Procedure:
1. Describe how paper is used in a classroom.

   _____

   _____

   _____

2. Is paper considered an example of technology? Explain.

   _____

   _____

   _____

3. Predict the number of sheets of paper used in a classroom in a day. _____

4. Keep track of the amount of paper used during one day in your classroom.
5. Record in the data table how much is used in one day.
6. Record in the data table how the paper was used.

Paper Use

Amount of Paper Used in One Day (Number of Sheets)	How Was the Paper Used?

Name: _____ Date: _____

Chapter Three: Product Life Cycle

Student Activity

7. Using the data collected from the class, calculate how much paper is used in a school week and a school year.

Amount of Paper Used

Amount of paper used in one day (number of sheets)	Amount of paper used in school week (number of sheets in a day x 5 days)	Amount of paper used in one school year (number of sheets in a day x number of school days in a year)

8. How much paper would be used in 12 years of school?

_____

9. What happens to the paper once it is used?

_____

_____

_____

_____

_____

10. Where does the used paper go when it leaves the school?

_____

_____

_____

_____

_____

_____

_____

Name: _____   Date: _____

Chapter Three: Product Life Cycle

Student Activity

Activity 3: Making Paper

Materials:

Paper – newspapers, paper towels, construction paper, tissue paper torn into small pieces

Newspapers   Apron or smock   Warm water

Wooden frame - old picture frames can be used

Wire or nylon screen wire to fit the frame   Staples or tacks

Paper Towels   Spoon to stir the mixture

Disposable aluminum pan or plastic tub – that the frame fits inside

2- Kitchen towels   Liquid starch – optional to make the paper firmer

Glitter - optional   Dried flowers – optional   Rolling Pin - optional

Procedure:

Making the Mold
1.   Attach the screen wire to the frame with the staples or tacks to make the mold.

Making the Pulp
1.   Spread newspaper over the work surface.
2.   Tear up 4 cups of paper into small pieces (the smaller the pieces, the better it works).
3.   Place them in the pan.

Name:_____   Date:_____

Chapter Three: Product Life Cycle

Student Activity

4.   Add warm water to cover the paper and let it sit.

5.   What happens to the paper?

_____

_____

_____

_____

The wood fibers in the paper separate to create the solution that paper makers call pulp.

Making Slurry From the Pulp
1.   Beat the pulp with the spoon until the fibers are separated and no large lumps remain.

Name: _____   Date: _____

Chapter Three: Product Life Cycle

Student Activity

2.   Add water until the pan or tub is about half full. This mixture is called a slurry.
3.   Optional: Add glitter or dried flowers to the slurry.

Setting Up the Drying Area
1.   Fold one of the kitchen towels so it is about 2.54 cm thick and the size of your screen. This will be the couching mound to dry your paper.
2.   Place the towel on the newspaper or a cookie sheet.

Making Paper From the Slurry
1.   Hold the paper mold, screen side up, over the slurry.
2.   Holding the mold—a hand on each side—lower it into the slurry at a 45° angle.
3.   Then turn the mold under the slurry so that it is horizontal to the tub.
4.   Move the frame in the slurry so the fibers are suspended evenly. The mold should be completely submerged.
5.   With the fibers still in motion, lift the mold straight out of the water.
6.   Hold the mold over the slurry so the water can drain out.
7.   As it is draining, gently shake the mold from side to side and forward and back to help the fibers settle smoothly. An even layer should be in the mold.
8.   When the water has drained, the edges can now be evened out with a ruler, or they may be left irregular.

Name: _____ Date: _____

Chapter Three: Product Life Cycle

Student Activity

Drying the Paper

1. Turn the mold over quickly onto the couching mound (towel) so that the paper is on the towel.
2. Slowly roll the mold from one edge to the other to loosen the sheet. (You may push on the screen to help release the paper. If necessary, you can use a spatula to help separate it.)
3. Place a towel (or layers of paper towels) over the top of the sheet of paper and press to absorb more of the water.
4. Optional: Roll the rolling pin firmly but gently over the paper to remove more water and flatten the paper.
5. Remove the top towel carefully

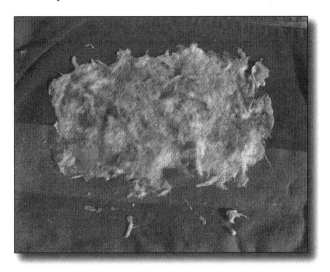

6. Let the sheet of paper dry several hours or overnight. It will dry faster if taken off the couching mound. Put it in the sun, or dry it with a hair dryer.
7. The color of the paper depends on what was put into it. Newspapers turn the paper gray, construction paper adds specks of color, etc.

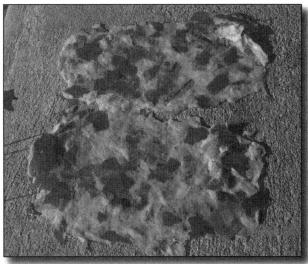

Name: _____   Date: _____

Chapter Three: Product Life Cycle

Student Activity

Results:

1. What resources were used in making paper?

   _____

   _____

   _____

   _____

   _____

2. What forms of energy were needed to make this paper?

   _____

   _____

   _____

3. What types of wastes were left from making the paper?

   _____

   _____

   _____

Conclusion:

1. How should the waste from making paper be disposed?

   _____

   _____

   _____

   _____

2. What were some of the problems with making paper this way?

   _____

   _____

   _____

   _____

Name: _____   Date: _____

Chapter Three: Product Life Cycle

Student Activity

3. Describe what a paper mill might be like if it makes tons of paper a day.

_____

_____

_____

_____

_____

_____

4. Why do you think recycling paper is important?

_____

_____

_____

_____

_____

_____

5. How is the new paper different from the paper that was recycled?

_____

_____

_____

_____

_____

_____

Challenges:

1. On your own paper, design a plan to reduce the amount of paper being used in your classroom.

2. On your own paper, design a plan to reduce the amount of paper used at home.

Chapter Three: Product Life Cycle

Further Investigation: Product Life Cycles and Paper

American Forest Foundation
http://www.affoundation.org/

American Forest & Paper Association
http://www.afandp.org/

EPA: Paper Recycling: Frequent Questions
http://www.epa.gov/osw/conserve/materials/
paper/faqs.htm#

Fun Science Gallery: Making and Recycling Paper at Home
http://www.funsci.com/fun3_en/paper/paper.
htm

Kids Gardening: Making Paper
http://www.kidsgardening.com/growingideas/
projects/nov02/pg1.html

Making Paper from Plants
http://www.missioncreekpress.com/plants.htm

Paper University
http://www.tappi.org/paperu/welcome.htm

Pioneer Thinking: Making Paper
http://www.pioneerthinking.com/making
paper.html

Project Learning Tree
http://www.plt.org/

Think Quest: Making Paper from Recycled Paper
http://library.thinkquest.org/4054/recyc/
pap.mak/papermaking.1.html

Weyerhaeuser: Growing Ideas
http://www.growing ideas.com/#/
WhatCanATreeBe/

Wisconsin Paper Council
http://www.wipapercouncil.org/

The Invention of Paper
http://www.wipapercouncil.org/invention.
htm

Paper Making Process
http://www.wipapercouncil.org/process.
htm

Paper in Wisconsin: Make Paper
http://www.wipapercouncil.org/makepaper.
htm

Paper in Wisconsin: Fun Facts
http://www.wipapercouncil.org/funfacts.
htm

Name: _____   Date: _____

Chapter Three: Product Life Cycle

Product Life Cycle Assessment

Objectives:

Students will be able to…

- Describe the life cycle of paper.
- Explain how energy is used in each stage of the life cycle of paper.
- Describe the resources needed to make paper.
- Explain the environmental impact of making paper.
- Conduct a life cycle assessment.
- Explain how paper can be recycled.

Matching:

_____ 1. Life-cycle assessment

_____ 2. Slurry

_____ 3. Mold

_____ 4. Pulp

_____ 5. Papyrus

a. Plant found in Egypt 5000 years ago; the leaves were harvested and turned into writing material; the word *paper* is derived from this word

b. Examination of all of the resources needed to make a product and the environmental impact of the product from its creation, use, and disposal

c. Frame with a screen used in making paper

d. A dilute water suspension of wood fibers

e. Solution made when the pulp is mixed with more water

6. Explain what a life-cycle assessment is. _____

_____

_____

_____

7. Why is it important to recycle paper? _____

_____

_____

_____

8. On your own paper, describe the life cycle of paper.

Chapter Four: Composting

Teacher Information

Topic: Composting

Standards:

NSES – Unifying Concepts and Processes
Systems, Order, and Organization
Form and Function

NSES – Content
NSES A: Science as Inquiry
NSES B: Physical Science
NSES C: Life Science
NSES D: Earth and Space
NSES E: Science and Technology
NSES F: Personal and Social Perspectives
NSES G: Science as a Human Endeavor

NCTM:
Problem Solving
Communication
Reasoning
Mathematical Connections
Probability

ITEA:
Nature of Technology
Technology and Society
Technological World

Concepts:
Solid wastes
Waste management
Recycling, reducing, and reusing materials
Getting rid of solid wastes
Composting
Decomposition
Organic material
Microorganisms

Objectives:
Students will be able to…
- Explain the requirements for the decomposition of organic materials.
- Explain the processes involved in composting.
- Describe materials that can be composted.

Activity: Composting (p. 47–53)

Materials: (Per group)
500 g Leaves, grass, small pieces of fruit and vegetable scraps
800 mL Garden soil (Do not use potting soil. It has been sterilized.) Compost from a compost pile can also be added instead of the soil.
50 mL Water
4 2-L bottles per group
Push pin or nail to punch holes in the plastic
5 x 5 cm square of gauze or netting
Rubber bands
Box cutter
Water
Graduate or measuring cups
600 mL measuring beaker or measuring cup
Large mixing container
Permanent marker
Ruler
Worms – optional
Cold and warm storage area – optional

TEACHER NOTE: Some variables that could be tested are temperature, moisture, exposure to light, amount of oxygen, acidity, adding earthworms, color of bottle, type of soil, type and amounts of fruits and vegetables, amount of garden soil or compost, etc.

Chapter Four: Composting

Student Information

Topic: Composting

Concepts:

Solid wastes
Waste management
Recycling, reducing, and reusing materials
Getting rid of solid wastes
Composting
Decomposition
Organic material
Microorganisms

Objectives:

Students will be able to…

- Explain the requirements for the decomposition of organic materials.
- Explain the processes involved in composting.
- Describe materials that can be composted.

Content Background:

Organic materials, such as yard trimmings, food scraps, wood waste, and paper, are the largest component of our solid wastes. They make up about two-thirds of the solid waste. Composting organic materials can help to reduce this waste. Composting can be done at home or even in an apartment, or it might take place at a city-wide composting site.

No matter how large a compost site is, it needs several things to turn, or 'cook,' organic waste into compost. First, a site needs to receive plenty of sunshine. The hotter a compost pile gets, the faster the material breaks down. Compost piles do best when internal temperatures are between 140° and 160° F. Organic wastes break down much faster during summer months.

Compost also needs water. A dry compost pile may take a year or longer to break down the material. On the other hand, a compost pile that is too wet won't cook, either. It'll just smell. One way to check on the moisture level of a compost pile is to turn it frequently. Turning the compost, either with a shovel or a pitchfork, will also ensure that enough oxygen gets to the center of the pile.

What can be composted? Organic materials the EPA recommends for composting include animal manure (excluding pet wastes), cardboard rolls, clean paper, coffee grounds and filters, cotton rags, dryer and vacuum cleaner lint, eggshells, fireplace ash, fruits and vegetables, yard clippings, hair and fur, hay, straw, houseplants, leaves, nut shells, sawdust, shredded newspaper, tea bags, and wool rags.

Most compostable materials can be divided up into two different categories. The first category is known as the brown category. The brown category is made up things like leaves, straw, shredded newspaper, cardboard, and nut shells—things that are usually brown in color. The brown category is high in carbon. Because browns are naturally drier, they require more water for the compost to cook.

The second category is the green category. This category is made up of grass clippings, fruit and vegetable wastes, coffee grounds, tea leaves, and even seaweed. The green category is high in nitrogen. The more greens in your compost pile, the less water you need for it to cook.

Chapter Four: Composting

Student Information

Brown Items for Composting

Mixing browns and greens in a home compost pile helps the pile achieve a hot temperature to help the decomposition process. It also helps regulate the amount of moisture a pile needs. With the proper temperatures and moisture levels, organic wastes can break down in as little as two months. However, even if it takes longer, that waste is still not a part of the waste stream.

Some things should not be composted. Black walnut leaves and twigs and coal or charcoal ash should not be used because they may have harmful substances that may kill other plants. Dairy products, fats, grease, lard, or oils and meat or fish scraps create odor problems and at-

Green Items for Composting

tract flies and rodents, so they should not be put into compost piles. Pet wastes should not be composted because they contain parasites, bacteria, germs, or viruses that may be harmful to humans. Lastly, yard trimmings that have been chemically treated may also kill the microorganisms that help decompose the compost.

The final product from composting is called **humus**. It looks and feels like fertile garden soil. Humus can be added to all kinds of soil to add nutrients to help plants grow better. Decomposing organisms, such as bacteria and fungi, and larger organisms, like worms, sow bugs, nematodes, and others, help break down the organic matter. These decomposing organisms need nitrogen, carbon, moisture, and oxygen to thrive. The organic materials provide most of these materials.

The two main kinds of composting are aerobic and anaerobic composting. **Aerobic composting** is composting in the presence of oxygen. The formula for the process of aerobic composting is: organic materials + oxygen + water = carbon dioxide + water + energy. This process allows the composting microbes that are aerobic (need oxygen) to help decompose the garbage and reduce the odor given off.

Anaerobic composting is composting without the presence of oxygen. The formula for anaerobic composting is: organic materials + water = carbon dioxide + methane + hydrogen sulfide + energy. This process will decompose the organic materials slowly, and the pile will smell of putrefying garbage.

There is a third type of composting called vermicomposting. **Vermicomposting** is composting that is speeded up by adding red worms. Worms help aerate the soil and help break down the organic materials as they eat the plant matter. Most experts recommend one to two pounds of worms for every one pound of organic waste you want composted.

Chapter Four: Composting

Student Information

Anaerobic composting is done in a closed container, while aerobic composting requires air.

Vermicomposting is popular in city environments because worms do not require hot temperatures to convert waste, and vermicompost bins usually have less odor than a regular compost pile. Worms do best in the same types of temperatures we enjoy indoors—55° to 77° F. Worms produce castings, which are full of nutrients that garden plants love.

Soil is a mixture of minerals from rocks and organic materials from decomposing plants and animals. The top layer of soil usually contains the most organic materials and nutrients. This layer is loosely packed so plant roots can penetrate the soil and draw out the nutrients and water to help

the plant grow. The lower levels of the soil are tightly packed and have few nutrients. Composting occurs naturally. In the woods, gardens, and lawns, natural composting happens when vegetation dies and falls to the ground. As it decays, it provides minerals and nutrients needed for plants, animals, and microorganisms.

Many compost experts call compost 'gardening gold' because of the benefits it brings to lawns and gardens. Compost works best in the top layer of soil. There, it helps the soil retain nutrients, air, and water, which helps plants survive dry or even drought conditions. Compost balances the pH of soil and helps protect plants from many common plant diseases. It also encourages beneficial garden animals like worms to stay in your garden.

Even people who live in cities can successfully compost. Vermicomposting takes up very little space—a small bucket will do—requires no temperature control, and produces very little odor. City gardens or even the trees in front of apartment buildings are happy to receive this compost.

Many cities have community organizations, such as the New York City Compost Project, that will help residents fit composting into their lives. They sponsor compost drop-off sites around the

45

Chapter Four: Composting

Student Information

Compost drop-off site

city where people can bring their organic wastes for composting.

San Francisco, California, is the U.S. city with the largest composting operation. San Francisco's goal is to keep 75% of its trash out of landfills by 2010 and reaching the point of zero waste by 2020. The people of San Francisco and local restaurants and food-related businesses produce more than 300 tons of organic garbage each day. San Francisco has mandatory curb-side pick-up of organic waste. This waste is taken to a composting facility and turned into compost. The compost is then sold to agricultural operations, such as vineyards, for fertilizer.

Community outreach is another part of San Francisco's larger plan. The city held large public events to promote the three R's of waste management: reduce, reuse, and recycle. San Francisco's overall environmental plan includes grants, subsidies, and other incentive programs for green activities, such as adding solar panels, planting trees, reducing greenhouse gases, and carpooling.

Boston, Massachusetts, plans to build a state-of-the-art indoor composting facility that will handle 75–150 tons of organic waste per day. This facility will decompose organic waste and collect the methane gas produced to power as many as 1,500 homes. The facility will also have a rooftop greenhouse sustained by the energy generated by the composting process.

In this chapter's activity, students will be designing and investigating a composter to determine the factors that will cause organic materials to break down more quickly.

Humus—the final product of composting

Name: _____ Date: _____

Chapter Four: Composting

Student Activity

Activity: Composting

Challenge Question: What factors make compost break down faster? (Factors to test include temperature, moisture, exposure to light, amount of oxygen, acidity, adding earthworms, color of bottle, type of soil, etc.)

Materials: (Per group)

500 g Leaves, grass, small pieces of fruit and vegetable scraps

800 mL Garden soil (Do not use potting soil. It has been sterilized.) Compost from a compost pile can also be added instead of the soil.

50 mL Water	4 2-L bottles per group	Push pin or nail to punch holes in the plastic
2 5 x 5 cm squares of gauze or netting		Rubber bands
Box cutter	Water	Graduate or measuring cups
600 mL measuring beaker or measuring cup		Large mixing container
Permanent marker	Ruler	
Worms – optional	Cold and warm storage area – optional	

Procedure:

Composter Construction

Make two composters from these instructions. One will be the control with no treatment, and one will be the test.

1. Use the marker to mark one of the bottles Control and one Manipulated.
2. Cut one of the 2-L bottles 10 cm from the bottom. This will be the base of your composter.
3. Cut the bottom off of the other bottle 6 cm from the bottom. This will be the bin of your composter. Keep the bottom as a lid. Recycle the other pieces.
4. Place the net or gauze over the mouth of the bin, and put the rubber band around it to hold it in place.
5. Place the bin in the base, with the mouth of the bin facing down.

NOTE: If you are testing green and clear bottles, use one clear and one green and do exactly the same thing to both of them. If testing the role of oxygen in the decomposition, construct an aerobic composter by using the push pin or nail to put 12 holes in the sides of the bin portion of one of the composters, and keep everything else the same.

Name: _____ Date: _____

Chapter Four: Composting

Student Activity

Compost Mixing

1. Mix 400 mL of garden soil, 250 grams of organic materials, and 25 mL of water in mixing container.
2. Place the mixture into the bin of your composter, spreading it evenly in the control composter.
3. Repeat for the second bin.

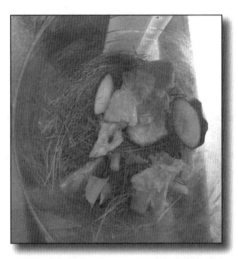

4. Measure the height of the column of compost in each composter and record the data.
5. Mark a line on the bin to show the starting height of the compost.

6. Record the starting height of each composter in the chart below.

Starting Height Control Composter (cm)	Starting Height Manipulated Composter (cm)

48

Name: _____   Date: _____

Chapter Four: Composting

Student Activity

Design the Investigation Test Conditions

1. Identify what variables might influence how fast the organic matter will decompose.

    _____

    _____

    _____

2. Identify the manipulated variable (the one that is being tested, i.e.: moisture, temperature, air). Note: Test one variable at a time.

    _____

3. Identify the responding variable (the one that responds to what is done).

    _____

4. Identify the variables you will be controlling (variables that are kept the same, i.e.: temperature, moisture, air, etc.).

    _____

    _____

5. Develop a hypothesis: If I _____

    _____ ,

    then the organic matter will decompose faster.

6. How will you know if it is deteriorating faster? _____

    _____

    _____

7. Record the procedures for the investigation. Procedures are step-by-step instructions of what will be done to the test composter. These need to be clear enough that someone else can follow them and do the same investigation.

    _____

    _____

    _____

Name: ______________________ Date: ______________________

Chapter Four: Composting

Student Activity

8. Draw and label a diagram of the investigation set up.

Name: _____ Date: _____

Chapter Four: Composting

Student Activity

9. Construct a data table to record observations. A sample table is below.

Controlled Composter Observations

Date	Height of Compost (cm)	Observations

Manipulated Composter Observations

Date	Height of Compost (cm)	Observations

51

Name: _____ Date: _____

Chapter Four: Composting

Student Activity

10. Construct a graph to represent the data collected. Put the controlled data in one color and the manipulated data in a different color on the same graph so that they can be compared.

Conclusion:

1. Under what conditions did the compost deteriorate the fastest? Explain the results.

   _____

   _____

   _____

   _____

2. Was your hypothesis correct? Explain why or why not.

   _____

   _____

   _____

   _____

Name: _____ Date: _____

Chapter Four: Composting

Student Activity

3. Do you have enough information to determine what factors influence how fast organic matter decomposes?

_____

_____

_____

_____

4. Is there anything else that needs to be investigated before the question can be answered?

_____

_____

_____

_____

_____

5. How could the investigation be redesigned to make the organic matter decompose faster?

_____

_____

_____

_____

_____

_____

_____

Challenges:
1. Redesign your composter to make the materials break down faster.
2. Design a compost pile for the school.
3. Research if your community composts its organic matter.
4. Design a plan to encourage people in your community to compost organic wastes.

Chapter Four: Composting

Further Investigation: Composting

California Environmental Protection Agency Integrated Waste Board: Closing the Loop
http://www.calrecycle.ca.gov/Education/curriculum/CTL/TOC.htm

California Recycles: Home Composting
http://www.calrecycle.ca.gov/Organics/HomeCompost/

Composting101.com
http://www.composting101.com/

Daily Dump: Composting
http://www.dailydump.org/composting

Earth 911: Composting in the City
http://earth911.com/news/2010/08/30/composting-in-the-city/

Earth 911: The Biology of Composting
http://earth911.com/news/2007/04/02/the-biology-of-composting/

Environmental Protection Agency (EPA)
www.epa.gov/

Composting
http://www.epa.gov/epawaste/conserve/rrr/composting/index.htm

Compost and Fertilizer Made From Recovered Organic Materials
http://www.epa.gov/epawaste/conserve/tools/cpg/products/compost.htm

Florida's Online Composting Center: Virtual Compost Pile
http://www.compostinfo.com/cn/Default.htm

How to Compost
http://www.howtocompost.org/info/info_composting.asp

How Stuff Works: How Composting Works
http://www.howstuffworks.com/composting.htm/

VegWeb.com: Introduction to Composting
http://www.vegweb.com/composting/

Natural Resources Conservation Service
http://www.nrcs.usda.gov/feature/backyard/Compost.html

Recology
http://recology.com/

San Francisco's Department of the Environment
http://www.sfenvironment.org/

Books

Appelhof, Mary. *Worms Eat My Garbage: How to Set Up and Maintain a Worm Composting System.* Kalamazoo, MI: Flower Press. 1997.

Campbell, Stu. *Let it Rot!: The Gardener's Guide to Composting.* North Adams, MA: Storey Publishers, LLC. 1998.

Gershuny, Grace, and Deborah L. Martin, eds. *The Rodale Book of Composting: Easy Methods for Every Gardener.* Emmaus, PA: Rodale Books. 1992.

Name: _____   Date: _____

Chapter Four: Composting

Composting Assessment

Objectives:

Students will be able to…
- Explain the requirements for the decomposition of organic materials.
- Explain the processes involved in composting.
- Describe materials that can be composted.

Matching:

_____ 1. Organic matter

_____ 2. Composting

_____ 3. Aerobic

_____ 4. Anaerobic

_____ 5. Decomposition

_____ 6. Decomposers

_____ 7. Vermicomposting

_____ 8. Humus

a. Microorganisms, such as bacteria and fungi, and larger organisms, like worms, sow bugs, nematodes, and others, that help break down the organic matter

b. Decomposes organic (was once living) waste using microorganisms, mainly bacteria and fungi, to break down the material into a usable form

c. Adding earthworms to the compost to speed up the decomposition

d. No oxygen

e. Oxygen is added

f. Any carbon-based material—plants and animals

g. Breaking down of matter

h. Decomposed organic material that looks and feels like soil

9. What do decomposing microbes need to survive?

_____

_____

_____

Name: _____   Date: _____

10.   Explain what requirements are needed for organic matter to decompose.

_____

_____

_____

_____

_____

11.   What processes are involved in composting?

_____

_____

_____

_____

_____

_____

12.   What kinds of materials can be composted?

_____

_____

_____

_____

_____

_____

_____

Chapter Five: The Five R's of Waste Management

Teacher Information

Topic: Reduce, Reuse, Recycle, Rethink, Re-buy

Standards:
NSES – Unifying Concepts and Processes
Systems, Order, and Organization
Form and Function

NSES – Content
NSES A: Science as Inquiry
NSES B: Physical Science
NSES C: Life Science
NSES D: Earth and Space
NSES E: Science and Technology
NSES F: Personal and Social Perspectives
NSES G: Science as a Human Endeavor

NCTM:
Problem Solving
Communication
Reasoning
Mathematical Connections
Probability

ITEA:
Nature of Technology
Technology and Society
Technological World

Concepts:
Waste management
Recycling, reducing, and reusing materials
Getting rid of solid wastes
Making decisions about what to do with solid wastes
Pollution
Environmental impact of waste

Objectives:
Students will be able to…
  • Explain why it is important to recycle, reduce, and reuse materials.
  • Explain why re-buying is an important part of waste management.
  • Explain why it is important to rethink how we live.

Activity 1: Reduce, Reuse, Recycle (p. 61–63)
Materials: (Per group)

List from day of trash	Ruler
Poster paper	Markers

Activity 2: Plastic Recycling (p. 64–65)
Materials:
All kinds of plastic

TEACHER NOTE: Try to find items from all seven of the plastic recycling categories.

The Daily Green website will provide information on plastics and recycling symbols.
http://www.thedailygreen.com/green-homes/latest/recycling-symbols-plastics-460321

Chapter Five: The Five R's of Waste Management

Student Information

Topic: Reduce, Reuse, Recycle, Rethink, Re-buy

Concepts:
Waste management
Recycling, reducing, and reusing materials
Getting rid of solid wastes
Making decisions about what to do with solid wastes
Pollution
Environmental impact of waste

Objectives:
Students will be able to…
- Explain why it is important to recycle, reduce, and reuse materials.
- Explain why re-buying is an important part of waste management.
- Explain why it is important to rethink how we live.

Content Background:

Waste management practices include recycling, composting, source reduction, landfills, and incineration. The EPA ranks the most environmentally sound solutions for solid waste. The most preferred method is source reduction, then recycling and composting, and lastly, disposal by incineration and landfills. In the United States, 33.2% of the waste is recovered and recycled or composted, 12.6% is incinerated, and 54% is put into landfills.

Source reduction is a way to reduce the materials needed to make products. It is the elimination of waste before it is created. **Source reduction** is altering the design, manufacture, or use of products and materials to reduce the amount of toxicity of what is thrown away as waste. Source reduction is a proactive way to reduce the need to collect, process, and dispose of trash. Grass-cycling, or mulching grass clippings, backyard composting, copying on two sides of paper, and reduc-

ing transport packaging by industry are examples of source reduction.

There are five R's in examining the issues involved in waste management. **Reduce** the amount of waste you produce. **Reuse** objects for new purposes. **Recycle** wastes into new materials. **Rethink** your values and your lifestyle. People may have to examine their values and decide what they are willing to give up in order to help improve the quality of the environment. The fifth R is to **re-buy** recycled products. When buying new things, look for the recycled materials symbol on the product.

Recycling turns materials that would be waste into resources. Recycling protects manufacturing jobs, reduces the need for landfill space and incineration, prevents pollution caused by the manufacturing of new products, saves energy, decreases emissions of greenhouse gases, conserves natural resources, and helps sustain the environment. Recycling removes glass, plastic, paper, and metals from the waste stream. Recycled materials are processed and manufactured into new products, and then they are sold. There are three steps to recycling a product: collecting and processing, manufacturing, and purchasing recycled products.

One example of recycling, **composting**, was investigated in the previous chapter. Com-

Chapter Five: The Five R's of Waste Management

Student Information

posting decomposes organic (was once living) waste (yard trimmings, food scraps, wood waste, and paper) using microorganisms, mainly bacteria and fungi, to break down the material into a usable form.

Incineration is another way to dispose of and recycle waste materials. **Incineration** is a controlled high-temperature burning of solid waste materials. This process helps reduce the amount of space needed for a landfill. The burning waste can be used to heat water to fuel heating systems or generate electricity. Burning waste at high temperatures destroys chemical compounds and disease-causing bacteria. Ash is monitored to be sure it is non-hazardous so it can be used for daily cover in landfills and road construction.

Some materials are degradable, renewable, and recyclable. What materials can be recycled are determined by how fast they break down (degradability) and how much it costs to recycle the materials. **Degradable materials** can be broken down by chemical, physical, or biological means. The materials in a landfill degrade slowly.

Renewable materials are things that can be replaced over and over again. Plants and trees are an example of a renewable material. **Nonrenewable resources** cannot be replaced in a short period of time. Ore, natural gas, coal, petroleum, and uranium are nonrenewable.

Recyclable items can be used to make new things. Paper, aluminum, steel, and glass are examples of recyclable items. The aluminum, steel, and glass can be melted down and made into new containers. Glass is one of the easiest materials to recycle, and it can be recycled over and over. However, many communities do not recycle glass, and many manufactures have switched to using plastic bottles instead of glass to reduce costs and breakage.

Most types of plastic can also be recycled. However, some plastics are not recycled because of the high costs of the recycling process. The numbers marked on plastic items identify how easy it is to recycle and how it can be recycled.

Plastic is found everywhere in cars, toys, packaging, clothing, home goods, utensils, medical devices, etc. Most plastics are marked with a recycling symbol with a number and/or letters identifying what the plastic contains. The type of plastic is determined by what is put into it or how it will be used. Plastics are classified into seven general categories. Some are accepted by community recycling programs, and some are not.

Plastics marked with the number 1 and/or PET or PETE in the recycling symbol are the most common plastics. They are made of polyethylene terephthalate (PET or PETE). They are found in soft drink and water bottles, peanut butter con-  tainers, and mouthwash, salad dressing, and vegetable oil bottles. This material can be recycled into polar fleece, tote bags, furniture, carpet, paneling, straps, and so on. It is inexpensive and easy to recycle.

Number 2 plastics are made with high-density polyethylene (HDPE). They are commonly found in milk jugs, juice bottles, butter and yogurt tubs, motor oil bottles, cereal box liners, some trash and shopping bags, detergent and household cleaning bottles, shampoo bottles, etc. This type of plastic can be recycled into new detergent bottles, oil bottles, pens, recycling containers, floor tile, pipes, lumber, benches, pet hous-

Chapter Five: The Five R's of Waste Management

Student Information

es, tables, and fencing. HDPE is versatile and has a low risk of leaching into the food supply.

Plastics marked 3 are PVC (polyvinyl chloride) or vinyl. Number 3 plastics are used for win-

dow cleaning and detergent bottles, shampoo bottles, clear food packaging, insulation on wires, medical equipment, siding, windows, and pipes. PVC is tough,

so it can be recycled into deck material, paneling, mud-flaps, road gutters, flooring, cables, speed bumps, and mats. It does contain chlorine, so the manufacture of this type of plastic can release dioxins that are harmful.

Number 4 plastics are low-density polyeth-

ylene (LDPE). Squeezable bottles, bread wrappers and frozen food containers, dry cleaning and shopping bags, tote bags, clothing, furniture, and carpet are made from LDPE. It can be recycled into trash can liners, cans, compost bins, shipping envelopes, paneling, lumber, and floor tile.

Polypropylene (PP), number 5 plastics, are found in some yogurt containers, syrup and ketchup bottles, straws, medicine bottles, etc. They

can be recycled into signal lights, battery cables and cases, brooms, brushes, ice scrapers, landscape borders, bike racks, bins, rakes, pallets, trays, and so on. Since it has a high melting point, it is used for containers for hot liquids.

Polystyrene (PS), recycle number 6, is found in disposable plates, cups, take-out boxes, meat trays, Styrofoam egg cartons, aspirin bottles, compact disc cases, etc. It

can be recycled into insulation, switch plates, egg cartons, vents, rulers, packing, and new take-out boxes.

Plastics with the number 7 include all other miscellaneous plastics. These take in all of the plastics that do not fit into the first six categories. Some are made from plants and are compostable, and some are made of polycarbonate, which is not compostable. Sevens are found in large

water bottles, bullet-proof materials, sunglasses, DVDs, computer cases, signs, some food containers, and nylon.

Re-buying recycled materials helps reduce solid waste in landfills and conserves resources. When consumers re-buy items made from recycled materials, they make it profitable for businesses to produce these goods. Without a market for recycled goods, manufacturers and waste handlers will not recycle materials, and they will end up in landfills.

The activities in this chapter will investigate the issues of reducing, reusing, recycling, rethinking, and re-buying waste materials.

Name: _____   Date: _____

Chapter Five: The Five R's of Waste Management

Student Activity

Activity 1: Reduce, Reuse, Recycle

Challenge Question: What would happen if natural resources ran out?

Procedure:

1. Select a day to keep track of the materials that you throw away. Record everything you throw away.

   _____

   _____

   _____

   _____

   _____

2. What is the difference between natural and man-made objects?

   _____

   _____

   _____

3. Examine the list of materials you threw out in a day.
4. Sort the items on your list into seven categories: paper, plastic, aluminum, steel/tin, glass, wood, and other.
5. Make seven columns on a sheet of poster paper, one for each category.

Paper	Plastic	Aluminum	Steel/Tin	Glass	Wood	Other

6. Record your trash on the poster paper table.
7. Were you able to categorize all of your trash?
8. Share your results with the class.

Name: _____   Date: _____

Chapter Five: The Five R's of Waste Management

Student Activity

9. Looking at the class data, which category had the most items in it? The least?

    _____

    _____

10. What items were the hardest to categorize?

    _____

    _____

    _____

Dilemma:

One of the things to consider in recycling and what goes into landfills is how fast a material degrades (breaks down).

How Long Does It Take to Degrade It?

Material	Time to Degrade
Styrofoam	Eternity
Glass Bottle	Unknown
Plastic Jug	1 million years
Disposable Diapers	500–600 years
Aluminum Can	200–500 years
Tin Can	200–500 years
Leather Shoe	40–50 years
Wood	10–15 years
Wool Sock	1 year
Cotton Rag	5 months
Paper Bag	1 month
Banana Peel	3–4 weeks

Other considerations are related to the item's form and function. What determines whether or not a material is used in manufacturing is the function of the product and the costs for manufacturing and transportation. For example, manufacturers use plastic and aluminum because these containers are

Name: _____   Date: _____

Chapter Five: The Five R's of Waste Management

Student Activity

lightweight and nonbreakable, which reduces the shipping and transportation costs. Glass is heavy and breakable, adding to costs. Glass jars and steel cans need paper labels. With aluminum, the label can be printed on the can. Less energy is used to manufacture plastic than aluminum. Plastic and steel use the same amount of energy. Consumers, the people who use products, seem to like plastic over glass and aluminum over glass and steel containers.

There are hidden costs and drawbacks to the use of each of these kinds of containers. Aluminum and plastics used by manufacturers for reduced costs may actually cause an increased cost for the consumer when they dispose of them. Plastics can absorb some of what is stored in them and can leach chemicals into foods and beverages. Aluminum and plastic can be punctured. A high percentage of litter is plastic, so taxpayers bear the cost of cleaning it up. Higher costs for using glass are in transporting the glass containers both from the manufacturer and when it is hauled for disposal.

Recycling rates are largely determined by four economic factors: dependability (having a consistent source of recyclables), material costs (expenses of sorting and collecting materials), manufacturing costs, and consistent demand for recycling and recycled products.

There are several drawbacks to recycling plastic. Federal health laws prevent reprocessing plastic into most food containers. There are 100 different kinds of plastic, and they cannot be processed together. Contaminants may interfere with the process. Plastic is also lightweight and bulky.

1. Who will pay for the use of non-recyclable containers? Manufacturers? Retailers? Consumers? Taxpayers?

    _____

    _____

    _____

    _____

2. What do we do with all of the trash we produce?

    _____

    _____

    _____

    _____

    _____

    _____

    _____

Name: _____   Date: _____

Chapter Five: The Five R's of Waste Management

Student Activity

Activity 2: Plastic Recycling

Challenge Question: How are plastics classified?

Materials:
All kinds of plastic (items from all seven categories of plastic)

Procedure:
1. Sort the plastics by symbols.
2. Examine each of the plastic items in each pile.
3. Identify the common characteristics.
4. Describe how the plastic was used.
5. Record the data in a data table. A sample table follows.

Item	Symbol	Characteristics	Use

6. Examine the data collected in the data table you created.

Name: _____   Date: _____

Chapter Five: The Five R's of Waste Management

Student Activity

7. How were the plastics in each category similar? How were they different?

    _____

    _____

    _____

    _____

8. How were the uses of the items in each category different?

    _____

    _____

    _____

    _____

9. Give an example of how the items in each category can be recycled.

    _____

    _____

    _____

    _____

    _____

    _____

10. Why do you think the plastics with the numbers 1 through 3 are more commonly recycled?

    _____

    _____

    _____

Challenges:
1. Design a way to use less plastic.
2. Design a way to reuse the plastics in your container.
3. Design a container that would provide the same benefits of plastic but reduce the use of plastics.

Chapter Five: The Five R's of Waste Management

Further Investigation: Reduce, Reuse, Recycle, Rethink, Re-buy

Association of Post-Consumer Plastics Recyclers
http://www.plasticsrecycling.org/

California Environmental Protection Agency Integrated Waste Board: Closing the Loop
http://www.calrecycle.ca.gov/Education/
curriculum/CTL/TOC.htm

The Daily Green: What Do Recycling Symbols on Plastics Mean?
http://www.thedailygreen.com/green-homes/
latest/recycling-symbols-plastics-460321

3 Suspect Plastics to Avoid in Baby Bottles, Water Bottles, More
http://www.thedailygreen.com/green-
homes/eco-friendly/plastic-bottles-toxins-
water-bottles-460410

Earth Odyssey, LLC: Recycling Symbols
http://earthodyssey.com/symbols.html

Education World: How Long Does Trash Last?
http://www.educationworld.com/a_lesson/03/
lp308-04.shtml

Environmental Protection Agency (EPA)
www.epa.gov/

Reduce, Reuse, Recycle
http://www.epa.gov/epawaste/conserve/
rrr/index.htm

Waste Reduction Through Conservation
http://www.epa.gov/epawaste/conserve/
rrr/reduce.htm

Wastes
www.epa.gov/epawaste/

Kids Recycling Zone
http://www.kidsrecyclingzone.com/

National Solid Waste Management Association: Recycling
http://www.environmentalistseveryday.org/
issues-solid-waste-technologies-regulations/
recycling-waste/index.php

The Plastics Web
http://www.ides.com/resources/
plastic-recycling-codes.asp

Project Learning Tree
http://www.plt.org/

Recycle Plastic Containers
http://www.sks-bottle.com/Recycle_Plastic.
html

Waste Management: Think Green
http://www.thinkgreen.com/recycle-what-
detail?sec=plastics&prod=plastic-recycling-
code

Name: _____   Date: _____

Chapter Five: The Five R's of Waste Management

Reduce, Reuse, Recycle, Rethink, and Re-buy Assessment

Objectives:
Students will be able to…
- Explain why it is important to recycle, reduce, and reuse materials.
- Explain why re-buying is an important part of waste management.
- Explain why it is important to rethink how we live.

Matching:

_____ 1.   Recycle #1

a.   Altering the design, manufacture, or use of products and materials to reduce the toxicity of what is thrown away

_____ 2.   Recycle #2

b.   Decomposition of organic wastes using microorganisms

_____ 3.   Recycle #3

c.   Use less so there is less waste produced

_____ 4.   Recycle #4

d.   Use a waste product for a new purpose

_____ 5.   Recycle #5

e.   Make waste materials into new materials by melting, etc.

_____ 6.   Recycle #6

f.   Reevaluate your lifestyle and values and how products are used

_____ 7.   Recycle #7

g.   Buy recycled products in the store

_____ 8.   Source reduction

h.   Most common plastic used; PET or PETE; easily recycled

_____ 9.   Composting

i.   HDPE; milk and juice bottles

_____ 10.   Reduce

j.   LDPE; squeeze bottles, frozen food containers

_____ 11.   Reuse

k.   PVC; detergent bottles, clear food packaging, pipe

_____ 12.   Recycle

l.   PP; yogurt containers, syrup and ketchup bottles

_____ 13.   Incineration

m.   PS; disposable plates, cups, take-out boxes, meat trays

_____ 14.   Rethink

n.   Other plastics

_____ 15.   Re-buy

o.   Burning of solid wastes to reduce the amount of space needed in the landfill

Name: _____   Date: _____

16.   Why it is important to recycle, reduce, and reuse materials?

_____

_____

_____

_____

_____

_____

17.   Why is re-buying recycled material an important part of waste management?

_____

_____

_____

_____

_____

18.   Why is it important to rethink how we live?

_____

_____

_____

_____

_____

_____

Chapter Six: Packaging
Teacher Information

Topic: Product Packaging

Standards:
NSES – Unifying Concepts and Processes
Systems, Order, and Organization
Form and Function

NSES – Content
NSES A: Science as Inquiry
NSES B: Physical Science
NSES C: Life Science
NSES D: Earth and Space
NSES E: Science and Technology
NSES F: Personal and Social Perspectives
NSES G: Science as a Human Endeavor

NCTM:
Problem Solving
Communication
Reasoning
Mathematical Connections
Probability

ITEA:
Nature of Technology
Technology and Society
Technological World

Concepts:
Types of packaging
Purpose of packaging
Need for packaging
Environmental impact of packaging
Making decisions about appropriate packaging

Objectives:
Students will be able to…
- Describe the purposes of packaging.
- Identify ways to reduce packaging.
- Explain what kinds of information are found on packaging.

- Identify materials used in packaging.
- Describe some ideas of how packaging could be reduced, recycled, or reused.
- Explain how excess packaging contributes to solid wastes.
- Design and construct packaging that serves the purpose of the packaging but reduces waste.

Activity 1: Purpose of Packaging (p. 72–73)

Materials: (Per group)
5 items in their original packaging – i.e., vegetables in plastic, electronic items in the package, shampoo bottle, chocolate bar, salad dressing, egg carton, etc.

TEACHER NOTE: The main purpose of this activity is for students to differentiate between the different materials used for packaging and the information the packaging displays. They also should find out what materials used for packaging are recyclable.

Activity 2: Packaging Design (p. 74–75)

Materials: (Per group)
A variety of construction materials – cardboard, plastic, paper, thin wood, cotton balls, cloth, etc.
6 of one kind of fruit (apples, peaches, oranges, cherries, etc.)

Chapter Six: Packaging

Student Information

Topic: Product Packaging

Concepts:
Types of packaging
Purpose of packaging
Need for packaging
Environmental impact of packaging
Making decisions about appropriate packaging

Objectives:
Students will be able to…
- Describe the purposes of packaging.
- Identify ways to reduce packaging.
- Explain what kinds of information are found on packaging.
- Identify materials used in packaging.
- Describe some ideas of how packaging could be reduced, recycled, or reused.
- Explain how excess packaging contributes to solid wastes.
- Design and construct packaging that serves the purpose of the packaging but reduces waste.

Content Background:

Packages in the past were refillable and made of reusable materials, such as glass bottles and cotton flour sacks. Some other materials used for packaging were baskets of reeds, wineskins, wooden boxes, pottery vases, ceramic and wooden barrels, and woven bags.

With new developments in technology in the early nineteenth century, processed materials were used to manufacture packaging from glass and metals, such as iron and steel. The emergence of the tin can in 1810 made it possible for food to have a longer shelf life. Glass bottles, such as soft-drink bottles, were returned to the store for cash back of a deposit paid at purchase. Paperboard and corrugated cardboard boxes came in later during the nineteenth century. Plastic has been used for packaging since 1960 because it is light, resistant to breaking, and can be made into any shape and color.

Currently, in the United States, most packaging is not reused but is discarded into the solid waste stream. During the twentieth century, the field of packaging grew into a huge industry. Packagers use materials like transparent glass, cellophane, aluminum, and plastic.

Packaging protects products during distribution, storage, sale, and use. Packaging has various functions. Manufactures need packaging to contain materials and protect and preserve what is inside. Consumers need to know what product is in the package, that the product is sanitary, and that the product is safe (i.e., child-proof caps). Packaging helps the manufacturers advertise and provide instructions on how to use the product. It also provides theft protection.

Chapter Six: Packaging

Student Information

Consumers can save money by purchasing products with less packaging because the more packaging, the more the manufacturer charges for goods. Consumers also can save money when less packaging ends up in the solid waste stream.

Each person in the United States discards several hundreds of pounds of packaging per year. Excess packaging increases the cost of items and the amount of waste generated. Some of the packaging contains non-biodegradable and toxic materials. Most litter found is from the packaging of goods and materials. This litter can impact tourism and harm or kill wildlife.

According to the EPA, one third of nonindustrial garbage in the solid waste stream is packaging. Twenty-eight countries now have laws to encourage manufacturers to reduce packaging and encourage more recycling of packaging that ends up in waste disposal.

Packaging can be made more sustainable by applying the principles of product stewardship: eliminate toxic materials in packaging, use less material, make packaging reusable, use more recycled materials in packaging, and make packaging so it is more readily recyclable.

Aluminum cans are easily recyclable, and reusable bottles cut down on waste sent to landfills.

One program dedicated to reducing packaging waste is Waste Wise, sponsored by the EPA. Waste reduction goals of these companies who choose to participate in Waste Wise are divided into primary packaging and packaging for transport. The primary packaging goals include waste prevention, recycling, and buying/manufacturing recycled materials.

Transport packaging can be reduced by using reusable containers dedicated to one product line, using incoming packaging materials for outgoing product, establishing preferred packaging guidelines for suppliers, using air-filled shipping cartons or biodegradable packing peanuts instead of styrofoam peanuts, and reducing the thickness of cardboard packaging material.

Wooden pallets are part of transportation wastes. To reduce this problem, companies developed a pallet return program. Pallets that could no longer be used are chipped up and used for animal bedding or compost. Other recycling strategies for transportation are to have package vendors use only one type of strapping, accept packaging materials from customers, purchase recycled wood pallets, and send the plastic shrink wrap to the manufacturer and buy back plastic containers made of it.

Packaging engineers consider the product and its package as elements of design. These engineers use the package to contain, communicate, carry, protect, and preserve the product. They develop the design and shape, then test different materials with the package design. The choice of material and the design can prevent waste in product packaging. Package engineers monitor post-consumer waste and source reduction.

This chapter will include identifying the purpose of different kinds of packages and what options there are in designing greener packages for a possible solution to the problem.

Name: _____   Date: _____

Chapter Six: Packaging

Student Activity

Activity 1: Purpose of Packaging

Challenge Question: Why are things consumers purchase put into packaging?

Materials: (Per group)
5 items in their original packaging – i.e., vegetables in plastic, electronic items in the package, shampoo bottle, chocolate bar, salad dressing, egg carton, etc.

Procedure:
Packaging has many purposes. Some include containing the materials, deterring the theft of the materials, keeping materials safe, keeping children safe from the materials, and advertising the product.

1. Choose one item from the pile.
2. Identify the purposes of the packaging on the item.

_____

_____

_____

3. Describe from what materials the packaging is made.

_____

_____

_____

4. Describe how much of the packaging is recyclable.

_____

_____

_____

5. How much energy and resources were needed to create this package?

_____

_____

_____

Name: _____ Date: _____

Chapter Six: Packaging

Student Activity

6. Look at the pile of packages. Is all of the packaging used really needed for each item? Explain.

   _____

   _____

   _____

   _____

7. Select an item that has packaging that could be reduced. Redesign the packaging to use less packaging or make it of recyclable materials. Be sure the new design serves the same function as the original. Draw your design below.

8. Examine the advertising on the packages. Describe what information can be found in the advertising.

   _____

   _____

   _____

   _____

9. Why is this information important to the consumer?

   _____

   _____

   _____

   _____

Name: _____ Date: _____

Chapter Six: Packaging

Student Activity

Activity 2: Packaging Design

Challenge Question: Can you design a package to keep fruit fresh?

Materials:
A variety of construction materials – cardboard, plastic, paper, thin wood, cotton balls, cloth, etc.
6 of one kind of fruit (apples, peaches, oranges, cherries, etc.)

Procedure:
1. Identify a fruit to package.
2. In your groups discuss:
   - What does the package need to do?
   - Who is the consumer?
   - How will the purpose affect the design of the container?
   - Three standards the packaging will have to meet: it needs to hold 6 pieces of fruit, attract consumers to buy it, and show the consumer exactly what is in the package.
3. Design a package for the fruit that will keep it fresh for the longest time.
4. Draw a diagram of your design.

5. Discuss in your group whether the design meets all of the criteria.
6. If not, how does it need to be changed to meet the criteria?

_____

_____

_____

Name: _____ Date: _____

Chapter Six: Packaging

Student Activity

7. When the fruit is transported, will additional packaging be needed? Explain.

_____

_____

_____

_____

_____

8. How could this packaging be improved?

_____

_____

_____

_____

_____

9. Draw a picture of the improved packaging.

Challenges:
1. Design a new package for something that you have purchased recently.
3. Identify what resources and energy were used in creating the packaging of something you have purchased. Then design a new package for this item that would use less energy and resources.

Chapter Six: Packaging

Further Investigation: Product Packaging

About.Com: How School Lunch Packaging Waste Adds Up

http://environment.about.com/od/greenlivingdesign/a/school_lunch.htm

Calculess: Environment Impact Analyzer

http://www.calculess.net/

California Environmental Protection Agency Integrated Waste Board: Closing the Loop

http://www.calrecycle.ca.gov/Education/curriculum/CTL/TOC.htm

Coca-Cola: Sustainable Packaging

http://www.thecoca-colacompany.com/citizenship/plantbottle.html

Earth Pack

http://www.earthpack.com/

Environmental Protection Agency (EPA)

http://www.epa.gov

Innovative Packaging

http://blog.epa.gov/blog/2010/03/25/innovative-packaging/

Pesticides: Topical & Chemical Fact Sheets

http://www.epa.gov/opp00001/factsheets/foodfyi.htm

Packaging

http://www.epa.gov/wastes/partnerships/stewardship/products/packaging.htm

Waste Wise

http://www.epa.gov/wastes/partnerships/wastewise/

Food and Drug Administration

http://www.fda.gov/

Recycled Plastics in Food Packaging

http://www.fda.gov/food/foodingredientspackaging/foodcontactsubstancesfcs/ucm093435.htm

Food Ingredients and Packaging Terms

http://www.fda.gov/Food/FoodIngredientsPackaging/ucm064228.htm

Package Design Magazine

http://www.packagedesignmag.com/

Packaging Law

http://www.packaginglaw.com/

Packaging Science

http://www.ist.rit.edu/~pscidrupal/

Paperboard Packaging

http://www.paperboardpackaging.org/

Project Learning Tree

http://www.plt.org/

The Responsible Package

http://theresponsiblepackage.com/

The University of Florida IFAS Extension: Consumer Choices Can Reduce Packaging Waste

http://edis/ifas.ufl.edu/ae226

Use Less Stuff

http://www.use-less-stuff.com/index.htm

An Ounce of Prevention

http://www.use-less-stuff.com/An-Ounce-of-Prevention.pdf

Waste Online: Packaging Recycling Information Sheet

http://www.wasteonline.org.uk/resources/InformationSheets/Packaging.htm

Name: _____ Date: _____

Product Packaging Assessment

Objectives:

Students will be able to…

- Describe the purposes of packaging.
- Identify ways to reduce packaging.
- Explain what kinds of information are found on packaging.
- Identify materials used in packaging.
- Describe some ideas of how packaging could be reduced, recycled, or reused.
- Explain how excess packaging contributes to solid wastes.
- Design and construct packaging that serves the purpose of the packaging but reduces waste.

1. Describe the purposes of packaging.

_____

_____

_____

_____

_____

2. What information is found on packaging?

_____

_____

_____

_____

_____

3. Why is the information on packaging important?

_____

_____

_____

_____

_____

Name: _____ Date: _____

4. Describe some of the materials used in packaging today.

_____

_____

_____

_____

_____

_____

5. How does excess packaging and nonreusable or non-recyclable packaging contribute to solid wastes?

_____

_____

_____

_____

_____

_____

_____

6. Describe ways that packaging could be reduced, reused, or recycled.

_____

_____

_____

_____

_____

_____

_____

_____

_____

Chapter Seven: Landfill Construction

Teacher Information

Topic: Landfill Construction and Environmental Impact

Standards:
NSES – Unifying Concepts and Processes
Systems, Order, and Organization
Form and Function

NSES – Content
NSES A: Science as Inquiry
NSES B: Physical Science
NSES C: Life Science
NSES D: Earth and Space
NSES E: Science and Technology
NSES F: Personal and Social Perspectives
NSES G: Science as a Human Endeavor

NCTM:
Problem Solving
Communication
Reasoning
Mathematical Connections
Probability

ITEA:
Nature of Technology
Technology and Society
Technological World

Concepts:
Landfills
Landfill construction
Solid wastes
Materials that go into a landfill
Leaching
Landfills take up space and reduce habitats

Objectives:
Students will be able to…
- Construct a model landfill.
- Explain how a landfill is constructed.
- Explain what materials go into a landfill.
- Describe solid waste.

Activity 1: Decomposition (p. 83–86)
Materials: (Per group)
2 large-mouth 64-ounce bottles with lids
2 L (about 2 qts.) Top soil
Plastic bag for cut vegetables
2 Straws   Paper   Pencil   Tape
2 L (about 2 qts.) cut-up fresh vegetables
1 piece cardboard cut into pieces
2 medium-sized plastic bags cut up
200 mL water   Ruler
1 qt. or 1L measuring cup

Activity 2: Toxic Wastes (p. 87–90)
Adapted from Center for Mathematics, Science, and Technology Education (1999) *Integrated Mathematics, Science, and Technology: Waste Management* – Analyzing Landfill

Materials: (Per group)
Two 2-L bottles
Mixture of 2 cups soil, 2 cups sand, and 5–6 small rocks
3 cups of soil in addition to the mixture above
Netting or gauze
Rubber band
1 plastic bag, one layer cut to fit the inside of the bottle (freezer bag or heavier plastic)
12 Gelatin capsules: fill each capsule with cornstarch (12 biodegradable packing peanuts can also be used if you can get a tight enough seal with the plastic); These are your toxic waste containers.
Iodine
Utility knife to cut the bottles
1,000 mL water
Measuring cup

Chapter Seven: Landfill Construction

Student Information

Topic: Landfill Construction and Environmental Impact

Concepts:
Landfills
Landfill construction
Solid wastes
Materials that go into a landfill
Leaching
Landfills take up space and reduce habitats

Objectives:
Students will be able to…
- Construct a model landfill.
- Explain how a landfill is constructed.
- Explain what materials go into a landfill.
- Describe solid waste.

Content Background:

In the past, garbage was just dumped into the streets. In 500 B.C., Athens, Greece, created a law prohibiting the dumping of garbage in the streets. They created the first municipal disposal site by requiring garbage to be dumped not less than a mile from Athens.

Careless waste disposal created problems because the piles of garbage multiplied as cities grew. This forced city governments to take on the responsibility of collection and disposal of garbage. At this time, they took the garbage outside of town and dumped it in open dumps. As cities grew, land where garbage could be dumped became harder to find, the odors became worse, and rats invaded the dumps for food. Some cities created open pits for garbage, but they found that these contaminated the groundwater.

In 1874, Nottingham, England, developed the first waste incinerator to burn garbage. The incineration took care of part of the problem of running out of space to put solid wastes, but it was costly and caused air pollution. In the 1900s, burying waste was the most common method of waste disposal.

The United States developed laws to protect human health and stop the pollution of navigable water-ways. The 1948 Water Pollution Control Act promoted research into the causes and solutions for water pollu-

tion. In the 1950s, there was an increase in solid waste because new technology led to new products and new packaging. This increase in solid waste created a need for trucks that compacted the garbage when it was collected.

The federal Solid Waste Disposal Act, 1965, provided money to study solid waste disposal methods. This study revealed the environmental impact and public health and safety issues resulting from landfills. From the 1970s to the present, more laws have been created to make landfills safer for people, animals, and the environment.

In 2008, residents and businesses in the United States produced 250 million tons of municipal solid waste or 4.5 pounds of waste per person per day. The EPA states that of the 250 million

Chapter Seven: Landfill Construction

Student Information

tons of waste, 31% is paper; 13.2% is yard wastes; 12.7% is food; 12% is plastic; 8.4 % is metal; 7.9% is rubber, leather, and textiles; 6.6% is wood; 4.9% is glass; and 3.3% is other materials.

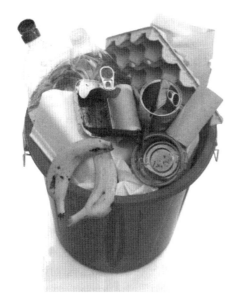

Examples of municipal solid waste (waste collected from cities) are product packaging, grass clippings, furniture, clothing, bottles, food, newspapers, appliances, paint, and batteries. When these items wear out or are replaced by something else, they become a part of the waste stream. A waste stream is the general flow of waste from the time it is thrown away until it is destroyed or buried. Some items are actually designed to wear out or fail after a certain time. This is called planned obsolescence. An example of planned obsolescence is car tires that must be replaced after a certain number of miles.

Waste management practices include recycling, reducing materials, reusing products, composting, source reduction, landfills, and incineration. The EPA ranks the most environmentally sound solutions for reducing solid wastes. The most preferred method is source reduction, then recycling and composting, and lastly, disposal by incineration and landfills. In the United States,

33.2% of the waste is recovered and recycled or composted, 12.6% is incinerated, and 54% is put into landfills.

When waste is thrown into a hole in the ground it is called a **dump**. Dumps create many environmental problems. **Sanitary landfills** are areas that have been specifically created to store solid wastes. Landfills are engineered to protect the environment from contaminants. The landfill siting laws prevent placing landfills in environmentally sensitive areas and provide for environmental monitoring systems that monitor groundwater contamination and the gases produced by landfills.

Modern landfills are constructed to prevent leachate from getting into the groundwater. **Leachate** is material that will pass or filter through the soil and can therefore get into groundwater, rivers, lakes, and streams. Clay soil and thick plastic sheeting can reduce the leaching of harmful chemicals into the groundwater. Piping and pumps are also installed to remove and treat the leachate before it builds up.

Landfills also need to be monitored for greenhouse gases. Landfills release methane, ni-

Chapter Seven: Landfill Construction

Student Information

trous oxide, and carbon dioxide. The total emissions are 2.25% of the U.S. greenhouse gas emissions. Some waste-to-energy landfills collect methane gas emissions to convert the gas to energy for heat and electricity. Other landfill facilities are using oxidation of the methane.

Recycling and composting reduced greenhouse gases by 2.5% in 2005. Eighty-five million tons of municipal solid wastes were recycled or composted in 2007. Between 1974 and 1997, increased recycling, composting, waste-to-energy sites, and landfill gas reduction have reduced the greenhouse gas emissions by 78%. This is a great improvement, but more needs to be done.

Landfills store carbon due to incomplete degradation of organic materials (containing carbon from living things) because these materials degrade slowly.

When selecting a landfill site, engineers must locate a site that meets local zoning and land use requirements. The site should be as close to the source of garbage as possible to reduce transportation costs. Engineers must look at not only the surface of the site but also the geological makeup under the site (**hydrogeologic setting**) to control pollution. Gas is the primary source of pollution. The gases must be vented or used as a source of energy for heat or electricity. The **aesthetics** (appearance) of the site must also be considered since it will be close to the community producing the waste. Landfill construction should also include landscaping, road construction, and odor control.

There are four components that make a safe sanitary landfill: a bottom liner, a leachate collection system, a cover, and the natural hydrogeologic setting. A properly designed landfill will not allow water from the landfill to seep into the water table. This can be achieved by developing a landfill in an area with **impermeable soil** (soil that

does not allow water to percolate or soak through the soil) or by placing liners under the wastes in the landfill site. These bottom liners may be one or more layers of clay or synthetic flexible plastic membrane. Waste is placed in the landfill on top of the liners, and then the waste is covered with soil every day. Over time, many layers of garbage and soil result. These alternating layers of soil and garbage decompose and are pressed tightly together to narrow the layers.

A methane gas recovery system allows methane gas, a by-product produced at a landfill, to be released into the atmosphere through the pipes that lead outside of the landfill. The gas can also be burned or used in energy recovery systems.

Leachate is water that is highly contaminated by wastes. It flows right to the bottom of a landfill and is collected by a system of pipes. The bottom of the landfill is sloped so that pipes laid along the bottom capture contaminated water and other fluids as they accumulate so they do not leak out into the environment.

Leachate Drain in a Landfill

In this chapter, you will be investigating what goes into landfills and how landfills are constructed.

Name: _____   Date: _____

Chapter Seven: Landfill Construction

Student Activity

Activity 1: Decomposition

Challenge Question: What happens to the solid waste in a landfill?

Materials: (Per group)

2 large-mouth 64-ounce bottles with lids   2 L (about 2 qts.) Top soil
Plastic bag for cut vegetables   2 Straws
Paper   Pencil   Tape   Ruler
2 L (about 2 qts.) cut-up fresh vegetables   1 piece cardboard cut into pieces
2 medium-sized plastic bags cut up   200 mL water
1 qt. or 1 L measuring cup

Procedure:

Step 1

1.   Mix the cut-up vegetables, plastic, and cardboard together.
2.   Add 2 cups of soil to the jar.
3.   Add four tablespoons of cut-up vegetables, plastic, and cardboard.
4.   Add 2 cups of another layer of soil.
5.   Add four tablespoons of cut-up vegetables, plastic, and cardboard, forming another layer.
6.   Add 2 cups of soil, forming another layer of soil.
7.   Add 200 mL of water to the top.
8.   Press down the materials.
9.   Measure and record the height of the pile.
10. Mark the starting height on the side of the jar with a piece of tape.
11. Cover the bottle and let it sit.

Image 1: Setup of Step 1 (layered soil and garbage mixture in jar)

soil

garbage mixture

soil

garbage mixture

soil

Name: _____   Date: _____

Chapter Seven: Landfill Construction

Student Activity

Step 2

1. Add 2 cups of the mixture of garbage into the other glass bottle.
2. Measure and record the height of the mixture.
3. Mark the starting height on the side of the jar with a piece of tape.
4. Cover the bottle and let it sit

Image 2: Stepup of Step 2 (mixture of garbage with no layers)

garbage mixture throughout jar

Image 3: The complete setup with all the tools needed

5. Insert 2 straws into each jar to allow the gas buildup below to escape. They can be inserted into holes in the lids of the jars, or cover the jars with plastic wrap and poke the straws through the wrap.

Image 4: Complete setup with the straws through the lids

Name: _____ Date: _____

Chapter Seven: Landfill Construction

Student Activity

6. Record your observations in a data table every 2 days for 30 days.

Date	Height (cm)	Observations

Name: _____   Date: _____

Chapter Seven: Landfill Construction

Student Activity

Conclusion:

1. What happens to the garbage?

    _____

    _____

    _____

2. Which materials decompose the fastest? The slowest? Or not at all?

    _____

    _____

    _____

3. Should organic materials be put into landfills? Explain.

    _____

    _____

    _____

    _____

4. Should plastic be put into landfills? Explain.

    _____

    _____

    _____

    _____

5. How should a sanitary landfill be constructed?

    _____

    _____

    _____

    _____

    _____

Name: _____   Date: _____

Chapter Seven: Landfill Construction

Student Activity

Activity 2: Toxic Wastes

Challenge Question: What happens to toxic waste in a landfill?

Materials: (Per group)
Two 2-L bottles
Mixture of 2 cups soil, 2 cups sand, and 5–6 small rocks
3 cups of soil in addition to the mixture above
Netting or gauze
Rubber band
1 Plastic bag, one layer cut to fit the inside of the bottle (freezer bag or heavier plastic)
12 Gelatin capsules: fill each capsule with cornstarch (12 biodegradable packing peanuts can also be
      used if you can get a tight enough seal with the plastic) These are your toxic waste containers.
Iodine
Utility knife to cut the bottles
1,000 mL water
Measuring cup

Procedure:
Landfill Construction
1. Cut the 2-L bottle 10 cm from the bottom. The top will be your landfill. The bottom will be the
   base.

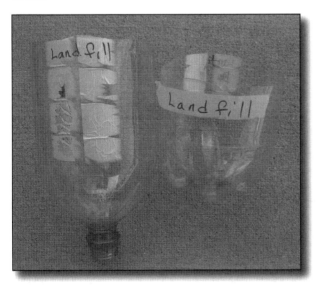
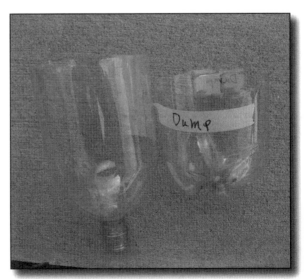

2. Place the net or gauze over the mouth of the bin and put the rubber band around it to hold it in
   place.
3. Place the bin in the base.
4. Repeat with the other 2-L bottle.

Name: _____   Date: _____

Chapter Seven: Landfill Construction

Student Activity

5.   Label one Sanitary Landfill and one Dump.

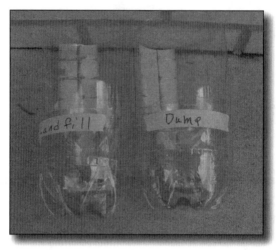

Sanitary Landfill Construction
1.   Place 2 cups of the soil/sand/rock mixture into the landfill container.
2.   Cut the plastic bag to fit the plastic bottle.
3.   Place the plastic on top of the soil/sand/rock mixture.
4.   Place 1 1/2 cups of plain soil on top of the plastic.
5.   Place the toxic waste—6 gelatin capsules filled with corn starch—in the soil.
6.   Cover with more plain soil

Dump Construction
1.   Place 2 cups of the soil/sand/rock mixture into the dump container.
2.   Place 1 1/2 cups of plain soil on top of the mixture.
3.   Place the toxic waste—6 gelatin capsules filled with corn starch—in the soil.
4.   Cover with more plain soil.

Name: _____   Date: _____

Chapter Seven: Landfill Construction

Student Activity

Experiment

1. Prediction: Will the landfill or the dump have more leachate (liquid material that filters through the soil) if water is added? Explain.

_____

_____

_____

2. Add 500 mL of water to each model. If the water goes through too fast, run the water collected in the base through again. It depends on how compacted your top soil is.

3. Let the models sit overnight.

4. Place 4–5 drops of iodine into the water (this represents the ground water) in the base to test for the presence of the leachate.
NOTE: If the "toxic waste" leachate came into the water in the base, the iodine should turn blue/black.

89

Name: _____ Date: _____

Chapter Seven: Landfill Construction

Student Activity

5. Which of the models had the most leachate in the base of the landfill container? How do you know?

   _____

   _____

   _____

   _____

   _____

   _____

6. Why do you think it had the most?

   _____

   _____

   _____

   _____

   _____

   _____

   _____

Challenges:
1. Visit a waste management site to see how the waste is handled in your community.
2. Design a landfill that will prevent leaching, consolidate wastes, not destroy habitats, provide energy for the community, and recycle all of the materials that can be recycled.

Chapter Seven: Landfill Construction

Further Investigation: Landfill Construction and Environmental Impact

The California Energy Commission: Landfill Gas Power Plants

http://www.energy.ca.gov/biomass/landfill_gas.htm

California Environmental Protection Agency Integrated Waste Board: Closing the Loop

http://www.calrecycle.ca.gov/Education/curriculum/CTL/TOC.htm

Environmental Protection Agency (EPA)

www.epa.gov/

Energy Projects and Candidate Landfills

http://www.epa.gov/lmop/projects-candidates/index.html

Landfill Methane Outreach Program

http://www.epa.gov/lmop/index.html

Landfill Reclamation

http://www.epa.gov/osw/nonhaz/municipal/landfill/land-rcl.pdf

Landfills

http://www.epa.gov/epawaste/nonhaz/municipal/landfill.htm

Transfer Stations For Non-Hazardous Waste

http://www.epa.gov/epawaste/nonhaz/municipal/transfer.htm

Environmental Literacy Council: Landfills

http://www.enviroliteracy.org/article.php/63.html

How Stuff Works: How Landfills Work

http://www.howstuffworks.com/environmental/green-science.landfill.htm/

National Solid Waste Management Association: Landfills

http://www.environmentalistseveryday.org/issues-solid-waste-technologies-regulations/landfills-garbage-disposal/index.php

Pew Center on Global Climate Change: Pattonville High School Landfill Gas Recovery Project

http://www.pewclimate.org/node/4112

Power Scorecard: Electricity From Landfill Gas

http://powerscorecard.org/tech_detail.cfm?resource_id=5

Rotten Truth About Garbage

http://www.astc.org/exhibitions/rotten/rthome.htm/

University of New Hampshire: Cogeneration Plant & Landfill Gas Pipeline

http://www.sustainableunh.unh.edu/climate_ed/cogen_landfillgas.html

WasteAge: Crystalline Vision

http://www.wasteage.com/Landfill_Management/crystalline_vision_lmop_lfgte/

Books

Center for Mathematics, Science, and Technology Education. *Integrated Mathematics, Science, and Technology: Waste Management.* Peoria, IL: Glencoe McGraw-Hill. 1999.

Illinois Department of Commerce. *4R's: Recycling Lessons and Projects: An Illinois School Teacher's Guide.* Springfield, IL: Illinois Department of Commerce and Economic Opportunity. 2009.

Name: _____ Date: _____

Chapter Seven: Landfill Construction

Landfill Construction and Environmental Impact Assessment

Objectives:
Students will be able to…
- Construct a model landfill.
- Explain how a landfill is constructed.
- Explain what materials go into a landfill.
- Describe solid waste.

Matching:

_____ 1. Dump

_____ 2. Landfill

_____ 3. Leachate

_____ 4. Solid waste

_____ 5. Planned obsolescence

_____ 6. Recycling

_____ 7. Source reduction

_____ 8. Composting

_____ 9. Liner

_____ 10. Hydrogeologic setting

a. Solid waste management facility designed for solid wastes that will also protect the environment

b. A hole in the ground where garbage is thrown

c. Material that passes or filters through soil

d. Items are designed to wear out after a certain period of time

e. Paper, yard waste, food, plastic, metal, rubber, textiles, wood, glass, etc.

f. Layers of clay and/or plastic sheets in the bottom of a landfill to prevent toxic fluids from leaking into the groundwater

g. Decomposition of organic wastes by microorganisms

h. Turns materials that would be waste into resources

i. Altering the design, manufacture, or use of products and materials to reduce the toxicity of what is thrown away

k. The geological structure under the location of a landfill site, i.e., groundwater, type of soil, and rock underneath the soil

Name: _____ Date: _____

11.   Describe what goes into a landfill.

_____

_____

_____

_____

12.   Draw a diagram of a good sanitary landfill.

13.   Explain how a good sanitary landfill is constructed.

_____

_____

_____

_____

_____

_____

_____

_____

93

Chapter Eight: STEM Design Challenge

Teacher Information

Topic: Design a solution for the disposal of solid wastes

Standards:
NSES – Unifying Concepts and Processes
Systems, Order, and Organization
Form and Function

NSES – Content
NSES A: Science as Inquiry
NSES B: Physical Science
NSES C: Life Science
NSES D: Earth and Space
NSES E: Science and Technology
NSES F: Personal and Social Perspectives
NSES G: Science as a Human Endeavor

NCTM:
Problem Solving
Communication
Reasoning
Mathematical Connections
Probability

ITEA:
Nature of Technology
Technology and Society
Technological World

Concepts:
Design a solution for the waste management problem

Objectives:
Students will be able to…
- Identify a problem.
- Brainstorm ideas about how you might solve the problem.
- Draw a diagram of the model.
- Construct a model of the solution.
- Test the solution.
- Evaluate the solution.
- Identify how to make changes to improve the design.
- Make the needed changes.
- Retest and reevaluate the design.
- Share the results.

Activity: Design Engineering Activity (p. 96–99)

Materials:
Variety of construction materials
Drawing paper
Markers

Chapter Eight: STEM Design Challenge

Student Information

Topic: Design a solution for the disposal of solid wastes

Concepts:
Design a solution for the waste management problem

Objectives:
Students will be able to…
- Identify a problem.
- Brainstorm ideas about how you might solve the problem.
- Draw a diagram of the model.
- Construct a model of the solution.
- Test the solution.
- Evaluate the solution.
- Identify how to make changes to improve the design.
- Make the needed changes.
- Retest and reevaluate the design.
- Share the results.

Content Background:

Environmental engineers try to solve problems related to air, water, and soil contamination. These contaminations may come from human activity or from the human use of technology. Humans need clean air, clean water, and good soil to live. One of the problems environmental engineers are trying to solve is how to dispose of waste products from homes, businesses, industry, and so on. Other problems are how to clean up water, air, and soil that are already contaminated.

Millions of people throw things into the trash every day. Some of that trash can become a valuable resource for new materials and can be put to new uses. There are five R's in examining the issues involved in waste management. **Reduce** the amount of waste you produce. **Reuse** the objects for new purposes. **Recycle** wastes into new

materials. **Rethink** your values and your lifestyle. **Re-buy** recycled products.

Attitudes of the people in the community will have an impact on the decisions being made about solid waste disposal. People may have to examine their values and decide what they are willing to give up in order to help improve the quality of the environment. The purpose of this book on managing wastes is to help students make informed decisions that will help them reduce, reuse, recycle, and rethink the ways waste is managed.

Integrated waste management is a system that combines multiple methods of solving problems related to handling solid wastes. An integrated waste management system could include waste prevention, recycling, landfills, composting, reusing, incineration, waste-to-energy facilities, and disposal sites for hazardous household wastes. The Environmental Protection Agency recommends using at least three strategies: source reduction, recycling, and burning wastes with energy recovery and landfill.

This book has presented multiple ways of managing solid wastes. The activity in this chapter starts with an examination of lifestyle and impact of attitudes and beliefs about lifestyle on how solid waste is managed. In this activity, students will conduct a solid-waste-management needs assessment, identify a problem related to solid waste management, and brainstorm ideas about how to solve the identified problem. They will then design a solution, test the solution, evaluate the results of the test, redesign the plan if necessary, and present the plan to the rest of the class for their evaluation.

Using what they have learned in this book, students will develop a sanitary waste plan that reduces the amount of waste, reduces natural resources used, reduces energy consumption, and reduces the impact on the environment.

Name: _____   Date: _____

Chapter Eight: STEM Design Challenge

Student Activity

Activity: Design Engineering Activity

STEM Challenge Question: Can you design a solution to waste management problems?

Materials:
Variety of construction materials
Drawing paper
Markers

Procedure:
     Your own attitudes and the attitudes of the people in your community will have an impact on the decisions being made about solid waste disposal. Examining your lifestyle is a good place to start. You can manage your own waste by reviewing your behavior, establishing a plan to reduce the amount of waste you produce, and implementing the plan. Take personal responsibility for reusing, reducing, recycling, rethinking, and re-buying recycled materials to reduce your own wastes.

Discuss in Your Groups
1. Does your lifestyle contribute to the waste problem? If so, how?

    _____

    _____

    _____

    _____

    _____

2. Survey students in your classroom to find out what percentage recycle. Based on your findings, are they contributing to the waste problem? Explain.

    _____

    _____

    _____

    _____

    _____

    _____

    _____

Name: _____   Date: _____

Chapter Eight: STEM Design Challenge

Student Activity

Develop a Solution

1. Using what you have learned in this book, develop a sanitary waste plan that reduces the amount of wastes, reduces natural resources used, reduces energy consumption, and reduces the impact on the environment. Include:
   - A description of the solid waste problem you are trying to solve
   - A plan to solve the solid waste problem
   - An explanation of how your solution will solve the solid waste problem
   - A diagram of any processing facilities—sanitary landfills, recycling centers, etc.
   - Presentation charts or diagrams for the class

2. Identify a solid waste problem below.

   _____

   _____

   _____

3. Brainstorm ideas about how you might solve the problem. Remember, during a brainstorming session, all possible solutions are recorded.

   _____

   _____

   _____

   _____

   _____

   _____

   _____

   _____

   _____

   _____

   _____

   _____

Name: _____   Date: _____

Chapter Eight: STEM Design Challenge

Student Activity

4.   Draw a diagram of your model.

Construct a Model of Your Solution

1.   Build and test your solution. Describe how you tested the solution.

_____

_____

_____

_____

_____

2.   Record your observations.

_____

_____

_____

_____

_____

Name: _____ Date: _____

Chapter Eight: STEM Design Challenge

Student Activity

Evaluate Your Solution

1. How well did the design work?

   _____

   _____

   _____

2. Identify changes that need to be made to improve your design.

   _____

   _____

   _____

   _____

   _____

3. Record any changes you made to the design.

   _____

   _____

   _____

   _____

   _____

4. Make the needed changes.
5. Retest and reevaluate your design.
6. Record your observations.

   _____

   _____

   _____

   _____

   _____

7. Share your results with the class.

Chapter Eight: STEM Design Challenge

Further Investigation: Environmental Engineering and Technology

Amazing Kids
http://www.amazing-kids.org/kids3-00.htm

California Environmental Protection Agency Integrated Waste Board: Closing the Loop
http://www.calrecycle.ca.gov/Education/curriculum/CTL/TOC.htm

Engineering Is Elementary: Engineering and Technology Lessons for Children
http://www.mos.org/EiE

Engineer Girl
http://www.engineergirl.org/

Engineering Challenges
http://www.engineeringchallenges.org/

Engineering K-12
http://egfi-k12.org/

Engineering, Science, and Mathematics Careers
http://www.khake.com/page53.html

Engineer Your Life
http://www.engineeryourlife.org/

Environmental Protection Agency (EPA)
www.epa.gov/

> **Landfill Methane Outreach Program**
> http://www.epa.gov/lmop/index.html
>
> **Waste Reduction Through Conservation**
> http://www.epa.gov/epawaste/conserve/rrr/reduce.htm
>
> **Wastes**
> www.epa.gov/epawaste/

Girl Scouts: Girls Go Tech
http://www.girlsgotech.org/engineer.html

Greatest Engineering Achievements of the 20th Century
http://www.greatachievements.org/

How Stuff Works Express
http://express.howstuffworks.com/

Inventions and Technology
http://kids.nypl.org/science/inventions.cfm

Inventions, Inventors, and You
http://www.ih.k12.oh.us/MSHERRMANN/Invent2.htm

Inventors and Inventions
http://edtech.kennesaw.edu/web/inventor.html

Kid Inventions: Inventions for School
http://inventors.about.com/od/kidinventions/ss/Young_Inventors.htm

Kids Konnect: Inventors and Inventions
http://www.kidskonnect.com/subject-index/15-science/86-inventors-a-inventions.html

Lemelson Center for the Study of Invention and Innovation
http://invention.smithsonian.org/resources/sites_teachers.aspx

National Academy of Engineers
http://www.nae.edu

National Center for Technological Literacy
http://www.nctl.org/

National Museum of Education: Invention
http://nmoe.org/students/index.htm

National Solid Waste Management Association
http://www.nswma.org

New York Public Library On-Lion: Inventions Changed Our World
http://teacher.scholastic.com/lessonrepro/lessonplans/theme/inventions.htm

Project Learning Tree
http://www.plt.org/

World Health Organization: Waste Management
http://www.wpro.who.int/health_topics/waste_management/

Waste Age: Profiles in Garbage
http://wasteage.com/waste-facts/

Books

Center for Mathematics, Science, and Technology Education. *Integrated Mathematics, Science, and Technology: Waste Management.* Peoria, IL: Glencoe McGraw-Hill. 1999.

Illinois Department of Commerce. *4R's: Recycling Lessons and Projects: An Illinois School Teacher's Guide.* Springfield, IL: Illinois Department of Commerce and Economic Opportunity. 2009.

Name: _____   Date: _____

 **STEM Design Challenge**

STEM Design Challenge Assessment

Objectives:
Student will be able to…
- Identify a problem.
- Brainstorm ideas about how you might solve the problem.
- Draw a diagram of the model.
- Construct a model of the solution.
- Test the solution.
- Evaluate the solution.
- Identify how to make changes to improve the design.
- Make the needed changes.
- Retest and reevaluate the design.
- Share the results.

Assessment of Technological Design:

Directions: Fill in the chart with information about the plan/model you made.

Technological Design	Indicator	Evidence
Identified the problem	Problem was identified	
Identified a possible solution for the problem	List of brainstorming solutions was provided and one solution was identified to test	
Constructed a model and plan for the solution	Plan states specifically what materials to be used and steps explaining how the materials will be used	
Tested the model and plan	Plan and model were tested, data was recorded	
Evaluated the model/plan	Results of the data were analyzed and the plan/model was evaluated, problems with the plan were identified, solutions to the problems were identified	
Redesigned the model/plan	Plan was redesigned to solve the identified problems in the first plan/model, and the new plan was tested and evaluated	
Communicated the results	Presented plans and results to other students	

Name: _____ Date: _____

Science Inquiry Skills Assessment

Basic Skills	Indicators	Evidence that students demonstrated process skill
Classifying	Grouping, ordering, arranging, or distributing objects, events, or information into categories based on properties or criteria, according to some method or system.	
Observing	Using the senses (or extensions of the senses) to gather information about an object or event.	
Measuring	Using both standard and nonstandard measures or estimates to describe the dimensions of an object or event. Making quantitative observations.	
Inferring	Making an interpretation or conclusion based on reasoning to explain an observation.	
Communicating	Communicating ideas through speaking or writing. Students may share the results of investigations, collaborate on solving problems, and gather and interpret data both orally and in writing. Use graphs, charts, and diagrams to describe data.	
Predicting	Making a forecast of future events or conditions in the context of previous observations and experiences.	
Manipulating Materials	Handling or treating materials and equipment skillfully and effectively.	
Replicating	Performing acts that duplicate demonstrated symbols, patterns, or procedures.	
Using Numbers	Applying mathematical rules or formulas to calculate quantities or determine relationships from basic measurements.	
Developing Vocabulary	Specialized terminology and unique uses of common words in relation to a given topic need to be identified and given meaning.	
Questioning	Questions serve to focus inquiry, determine prior knowledge, and establish purposes or expectations for an investigation. An active search for information is promoted when questions are used.	
Using Cues	Key words and symbols convey significant meaning in messages. Organizational patterns facilitate comprehension of major ideas. Graphic features clarify textual information.	

Name: _____ Date: _____

Science Inquiry Skills Assessment

Integrated Skills	Indicators	Evidence that students demonstrated process skill
Creating Models	Displaying information by means of graphic illustrations or other multisensory representations.	
Formulating Hypotheses	Stating or constructing a statement that is testable about what is thought to be the expected outcome of an experiment (based on reasoning).	
Generalizing	Drawing general conclusions from particulars.	
Identifying & Controlling Variables	Recognizing the characteristics of objects or factors in events that are constant or change under different conditions and that can affect an experimental outcome, keeping most variables constant while manipulating only one (the independent) variable.	
Defining Operationally	Stating how to measure a variable in an experiment; defining a variable according to the actions or operations to be performed on or with it.	
Recording & Interpreting Data	Collecting bits of information about objects and events that illustrate a specific situation, organizing and analyzing data that have been obtained, and drawing conclusions from it by determining apparent patterns or relationships in the data.	
Making Decisions	Identifying alternatives and choosing a course of action from among alternatives after basing the judgment for the selection on justifiable reasons.	
Experimenting	Being able to conduct an experiment, including asking an appropriate question, stating a hypothesis, identifying and controlling variables, operationally defining those variables, designing a "fair" experiment, and interpreting the results of an experiment.	

Name: _____ Date: _____

Assessment of Technological Design

TEACHER NOTE: Use this rubric to assess the design of any of the models in the chapter activities.

Objectives:
Student will be able to…
- Identify a problem.
- Brainstorm ideas about how you might solve the problem.
- Draw a diagram of the model.
- Construct a model of the solution.
- Test the solution.
- Evaluate the solution.
- Identify how to make changes to improve the design.
- Make the needed changes.
- Retest and reevaluate the design.
- Share the results.

Assessment of Technological Design:

Directions: Fill in the chart with information about the plan/model you made.

Technological Design	Indicator	Evidence
Identified the problem	Problem was identified	
Identified a possible solution for the problem	List of brainstorming solutions was provided and one solution was identified to test	
Constructed a model and plan for the solution	Plan states specifically what materials to be used and steps explaining how the materials will be used	
Tested the model and plan	Plan and model were tested, data was recorded	
Evaluated the model/plan	Results of the data were analyzed and the plan/model was evaluated, problems with the plan were identified, solutions to the problems were identified	
Redesigned the model/plan	Plan was redesigned to solve the identified problems in the first plan/model, and the new plan was tested and evaluated	
Communicated the results	Presented plans and results to other students	

Science Process Skills

	Skills	Definition
B	Classifying	Grouping, ordering, arranging, or distributing objects, events, or information into categories based on properties or criteria, according to some method or system.
A	Observing	Using the senses (or extensions of the senses) to gather information about an object or event.
S	Measuring	Using both standard and nonstandard measures or estimates to describe the dimensions of an object or event. Making quantitative observations.
I		
C	Inferring	Making an interpretation or conclusion based on reasoning to explain an observation.
	Communicating	Communicating ideas through speaking or writing. Students may share the results of investigations, collaborate on solving problems, and gather and interpret data both orally and in writing. Use graphs, charts, and diagrams to describe data.
P		
R		
O	Predicting	Making a forecast of future events or conditions in the context of previous observations and experiences.
C		
E	Manipulating Materials	Handling or treating materials and equipment skillfully and effectively.
S		
S	Replicating	Performing acts that duplicate demonstrated symbols, patterns, or procedures.
	Using Numbers	Applying mathematical rules or formulas to calculate quantities or determine relationships from basic measurements.
S		
K	Developing Vocabulary	Specialized terminology and unique uses of common words in relation to a given topic need to be identified and given meaning.
I		
L	Questioning	Questions serve to focus inquiry, determine prior knowledge, and establish purposes or expectations for an investigation. An active search for information is promoted when questions are used.
L		
S		
	Using Cues	Key words and symbols convey significant meaning in messages. Organizational patterns facilitate comprehension of major ideas. Graphic features clarify textual information.

I	Creating Models	Displaying information by means of graphic illustrations or other multisensory representations.
N	Formulating Hypotheses	Stating or constructing a statement that is testable about what is thought to be the expected outcome of an experiment (based on reasoning).
T		
E	Generalizing	Drawing general conclusions from particulars.
G	Identifying & Controlling Variables	Recognizing the characteristics of objects or factors in events that are constant or change under different conditions and that can affect an experimental outcome, keeping most variables constant while manipulating only one (the independent) variable.
R		
A		
T	Defining Operationally	Stating how to measure a variable in an experiment; defining a variable according to the actions or operations to be performed on or with it.
E		
D	Recording & Interpreting Data	Collecting bits of information about objects and events that illustrate a specific situation, organizing and analyzing data that have been obtained, and drawing conclusions from it by determining apparent patterns or relationships in the data.
S		
K	Making Decisions	Identifying alternatives and choosing a course of action from among alternatives after basing the judgment for the selection on justifiable reasons.
I		
L	Experimenting	Being able to conduct an experiment, including asking an appropriate question, stating a hypothesis, identifying and controlling variables, operationally defining those variables, designing a "fair" experiment, and interpreting the results of an experiment.
L		
S		

NSES Content Standards

Summary from the NRC (1996). *National Science Education Standards.* Washington, D.C.: National Academy Press.

Assumptions:
1. NSES Standards require changes throughout the system.
2. What students learn is influenced by how they are taught.
3. Actions of teachers are deeply influenced by their perceptions of science as an enterprise and as a subject to be taught and learned.
4. Student understanding is actively constructed through individual and social processes.
5. Actions of teachers are deeply influenced by their understanding of and relationships with students.

NSES Unifying Concepts and Processes:
Systems, Order, and Organization
Evidence, Models, and Explanations
Change, Constancy, and Measurement
Evolution and Equilibrium
Form and Function

NSES Content Standards:

Standard	Understanding	Indicators Grades 5–8 Students will be able to:
A. Science as Inquiry	Abilities to do scientific inquiry	Identify questions that can be answered through investigations.
		Plan and conduct a scientific investigation.
		Use appropriate tools and techniques to gather, analyze, and interpret data.
		Develop descriptions, explanations, predictions, and models using evidence.
		Think critically and logically to make the relationships between evidence and explanations.
		Recognize and analyze alternative explanations and predictions.
		Communicate scientific procedures and explanations.
		Use mathematics in all aspects of inquiry.
	Understanding scientific inquiry	Explain that different kinds of investigations are needed depending on the questions they are trying to answer.
		Explain that current scientific knowledge guides scientific investigations.
		Explain that mathematics is important to all aspects of inquiry.
		Explain that technology used to gather data increases accuracy and quantifies the results.
		Explain that scientists develop explanations from evidence from investigations and scientific knowledge.
		Explain that science advances through skepticism.
		Explain that scientific investigations may result in new ideas and investigations.

B. Physical Science	Properties and changes in properties of matter	Explain that substances have characteristic properties.
		Explain that substances react chemically in characteristic ways with other substances to form new substances (compounds) with different properties. Mass is conserved in chemical reactions.
		Explain that chemical elements do not break down during normal laboratory reactions. There are over 100 known elements that combine to form compounds.
	Motions and forces	Explain that motion can be described by its position, speed, and direction, and it can be measured.
		Explain an object in motion will move at a constant speed in a straight line until acted upon by another force.
		Explain if more than one force acts upon an object along a straight line, the forces either reinforce or cancel one another. Unbalanced forces will cause changes in the speed or direction of the motion.
	Transfer of energy	Explain that energy is a property of many substances and is transferred in many ways.
		Explain that heat moves in predictable ways, flowing from warmer to cooler areas until the temperature is equalized.
		Explain that light interacts with matter by transmission (including refraction), absorption, and scattering (including reflection).
		Explain that electrical circuits are a means of transferring electrical energy.
		Explain that in most chemical and nuclear reactions energy is transferred into or out of a system.
		Explain that the sun is a major source of energy for changes on the earth's surface. The sun's energy arrives as light with a range of wavelengths—visible light, infrared, ultraviolet radiation.
C. Life Science	Structure and function of living systems	Explain that living systems demonstrate the complementary nature of function and structure. Levels of organization include cell, tissue, organ, systems, organism, and ecosystems.
		Explain that all organisms are composed of cells.
		Explain that cells carry on functions needed to sustain life, they grow and divide, take in nutrients, and get rid of wastes.
		Explain that specialized cells perform special functions. Groups of specialized cells make tissues; groups of specialized tissues form organs.
		Explain that humans have systems for digestion, respiration, reproduction, circulation, excretion, movement, control and coordination, and protection from diseases.
		Explain that disease is a breakdown in structures or functions of an organism.
	Reproduction and heredity	Explain that reproduction is a characteristic of all living systems.
		Explain in many species females produce eggs and males produce sperm. Egg and sperm unite to form a new organism. The new organism receives genetic information from the male and female.

		Explain that organisms require a set of instructions to specify its traits. Heredity is the passage of these instructions from one generation to another.
		Explain heredity information is contained in the genes in the chromosomes of each cell. A gene carries a single unit of information. Inherited traits are determined by the genes.
		Explain that characteristics of an organism are from the combination of traits. Some traits are inherited and some are from interactions with the environment.
	Regulation and behavior	Explain that all organisms must be able to obtain and use resources, grow, reproduce, and maintain stable internal conditions in a constantly changing environment.
		Explain that regulation of the internal environment involves sensing the environment and changing physiological activities to keep conditions within the range required to survive.
		Explain that behavior is one kind of response an organism makes to an internal or external stimulus.
		Explain that an organism's behavior evolves through adaptation to its environment.
	Populations and ecosystems	Describe a population as all individuals of a species that occur at a given place in a given time. An ecosystem is all populations and the physical factors with which they interact.
		Explain that populations can be categorized by the function they serve in an ecosystem—producers, consumers, decomposers. Food webs identify the relationships among organisms.
		Explain that the major source of energy in an ecosystem is sunlight.
		Explain that the number of organisms in an ecosystem depends on the resources available and abiotic factors.
	Diversity and adaptations of organisms	Explain that millions of species are alive today.
		Explain that biological evolution accounts for the diversity of species.
		Explain that extinction of a species occurs when an environment changes and it cannot adapt.
D. Earth Science	Structure of the earth system	Describe that the earth is layered with a lithosphere (crust), hot convecting mantle, and dense metal core.
		Explain that lithospheric (crustal) plates constantly move in response to movements in the mantle.
		Explain that landforms result from constructive and destructive forces.
		Describe the rock cycle as some of the changes in the solid earth.
		Describe soil as weathered rocks and decomposed organic matter.
		Explain that water covers the majority of the earth and it circulates through the crust, water, and atmosphere (water cycle).
		Explain that water is a solvent and dissolves minerals and gases as it passes through the water cycle.

		Explain that the atmosphere is a mixture of nitrogen, oxygen, and trace gases.
		Explain that clouds are formed by condensation.
		Explain that global patterns of atmospheric movement influence local weather.
		Explain that living organisms play many roles in the earth system.
	Earth's history	Explain that earth processes—erosion, movement of plates, and changes in the atmosphere—also occurred in the past.
		Explain that fossils provide evidence of the past.
	Earth in the solar system	Explain that the earth is the third planet from the sun in the solar system. The sun is an average star and is the central and largest body in the solar system.
		Explain most objects in the solar system are in regular predictable motion.
		Explain that gravity is the force that keeps planets in orbit around the sun. It holds everything on earth and controls the tides.
		Explain that the sun is the major source of energy for phenomena on the earth's surface.
E. Science and Technology	Abilities of technological design	Identify appropriate problems for technological design.
		Design a solution or product.
		Implement a proposed design.
		Evaluate completed designs or products.
		Communicate the process of technological design.
	Understanding of technological design	Explain that scientists propose explanations for the natural world. Engineers propose solutions relating to human needs, problems, and aspirations. Technological solutions are temporary; exist within nature so they can not contravene physical or biological principles; solutions may have side effects and costs, carry risks, and provide benefits.
		Explain many different people from many cultures have contributed to science and technology.
		Explain that science drives technology, and technology is essential to science.
		Explain that designed solutions are not perfect; they have trade-offs and risks.
		Explain that technological designs have constraints.
		Explain that technological solutions have intended benefits and unintended consequences.
F. Personal and Social Perspectives	Personal health	Regular exercise is important to maintain and improve health.
		Potential for accidents and hazards create a need for injury prevention.
		Use of tobacco increases the risk of illness.
		Alcohol and other drugs are often abused substances.
		Food provides energy and nutrients for growth and development.
		Sex drive is a natural human function that needs understanding.

		Natural environments may contain substances that are harmful to human beings.
	Populations, resources, and environments	Overpopulated environments will become degraded due to increased use of resources.
		Causes of environmental degradation and resources vary.
	Natural hazards	Internal and external processes of the earth cause natural hazards.
		Human activities can also cause natural hazards.
		Natural hazards can present personal and societal changes.
	Risks and benefits	Risk analysis considers the type of hazard and estimates the number of people that might be exposed and the number likely to suffer consequences.
		Risks are associated with natural hazards, chemical hazards, biological hazards, social hazards, and personal hazards.
		A systematic approach should be used for risk benefit analysis.
		Personal and social decisions are made based on perceptions of risks and benefits.
	Science and technology in society	Science influences society through its knowledge and world view.
		Societal challenges often inspire questions for scientific research and social priorities influence research through availability of funding.
		Technology influences society through its products and processes.
		Science and technology have advanced through different people in different cultures in different times in history.
		Scientists and engineers work in different settings.
		Scientists and engineers have ethical codes.
		Science cannot answer all questions and technology cannot solve all problems.
G. History and Nature of Science	Science as a human endeavor	People of diverse backgrounds engage in science, engineering, and related fields.
		Science requires different abilities.
	The nature of science	Scientists formulate and test explanations using observations, experiments, and theoretical and mathematic models.
		Scientists may have different opinions.
		Scientific inquiry includes evaluating results of investigations, experiments, observations, theoretical models, and explanations of other scientists.
	The history of science	Many individuals have contributed to the traditions of science.
		Science has been practiced by different individuals in different cultures.
		History shows how difficult it was for scientific innovators to break through the accepted ideas of their times.

Principles and Standards for School Mathematics 5–8 (NCTM)

National Council for Teachers of Mathematics. (2000). *Principles and Standards for School Mathematics.* Reston, VA: National Council for Teachers of Mathematics.

Standard	Indicators
Problem Solving	Use problem-solving approaches to investigate and understand mathematics.
	Formulate problems from situations.
	Develop and apply a variety of strategies to solve problems.
	Verify and interpret results.
	Generalize solutions and strategies to new problems.
	Acquire confidence in using mathematics.
Communication	Model situations using oral, written, concrete, pictorial, graphical, and algebraic methods.
	Reflect on and clarify their own thinking about mathematical ideas and situations.
	Develop common understandings of mathematical ideas.
	Use the skills of reading, listening, and viewing to interpret and evaluate mathematical ideas.
	Discuss mathematical ideas and make conjectures and arguments.
	Appreciate the value of mathematical notation.
Reasoning	Recognize and apply deductive and inductive reasoning.
	Use reasoning processes.
	Make and evaluate conjectures and arguments.
	Validate their own thinking.
	Appreciate the pervasive use and power of reasoning as a part of mathematics.
Mathematical Connections	See mathematics as an integrated whole.
	Explore problems and describe results using graphs; numbers; and physical, algebraic, and verbal models or representations.
	Use a mathematical idea to further their understanding of mathematics.
	Apply mathematical thinking and modeling to solve problems.
	Value the role of mathematics in our culture and society.
Number and Number Relationships	Use numbers in a variety of forms.
	Develop number sense.
	Use ratios, proportions, and percents in a variety of situations.
	Investigate relationships among fractions, decimals, and percents.
	Represent numerical relationships on graphs.
Number Systems/ Number Theory	Understand the need for numbers beyond whole numbers.
	Develop and use order relations.
	Extend understanding of whole number operations to fractions, decimals, integers, and rational numbers.
	Understand how basic arithmetic operations are related to one another.
	Develop and apply number theory in real-world problems.
Computation and Estimation	Compute with whole numbers, fractions, decimals, integers, and rational numbers.
	Develop, analyze, and explain methods for computation and estimation.
	Select and use appropriate methods for computing.
	Use computation, estimation, and proportions to solve problems.
	Use estimation to check reasonableness.

Patterns and Functions	Describe, extend, analyze, and create patterns.
	Describe and represent relationships with tables, graphs, and rules.
	Analyze functional relationships to explain how a change in one changes another.
	Use patterns and functions to represent and solve problems.
Algebra	Understand variables, expressions, and equations.
	Represent situations and number patterns with tables, graphs, verbal rules, and equations and their interrelationships.
	Analyze tables and graphs to identify properties and relationships.
	Develop confidence in solving linear equations.
	Investigate inequalities and nonlinear equations.
	Apply algebraic methods to solve problems.
Statistics	Systematically collect, organize, and describe data.
	Construct, read, and interpret tables, graphs, and charts.
	Make inferences and arguments based on data analysis.
	Evaluate arguments based on data analysis.
	Develop appreciation for statistical methods for decision making.
Probability	Model situations by devising and carrying out experiments or simulations to determine probabilities.
	Model situations by constructing a sample space to determine probabilities.
	Appreciate the power of using a probability model.
	Make predictions based on experimental or theoretical probabilities.
	Develop an appreciation for the use of probability in the real world.
Geometry	Identify, describe, compare, and classify geometric figures.
	Visualize and represent geometric figures.
	Explore transformations of geometric figures.
	Represent and solve problems using geometric figures.
	Understand and apply geometric properties and relationships.
	Develop appreciation of geometry as a means of describing the physical world.
Measurement	Extend understanding of processes of measurement.
	Estimate, make, and use measurement to describe and compare phenomena.
	Select appropriate units and tools.
	Understand the structure and use of measurement systems.
	Understand perimeter, area, volume, angle measurement, capacity, weight, and mass.
	Develop concepts of rate and other derived and indirect measurements.
	Develop formulas and procedures for determining measures to solve problems.

ITEA Standards for Technological Literacy

Adapted from: International Technology Education Association (2007) *Standards for Technological Literacy*. Reston, VA: International Technology Education Association. URL: www.iteaconnect.org

Standards for Technological Literacy:

Goal	Standard	Grades 6–8 Indicators
Students will develop an understanding of the Nature of Technology.	Students will develop understanding of:	Students will be able to:
	1. Characteristics and scope of technology	Explain that new products and systems can be developed to solve problems or help do things that could not be done without the help of technology.
		Explain that technology is a human activity and is the result of individual and collective needs and the ability to be creative.
		Explain that technology is closely linked to creativity which has resulted in innovation.
		Explain that corporations can create a demand for a product by bringing it onto a market and advertising it.
	2. Core concepts of technology	Describe that technological systems include input, processes, output, and feedback.
		Explain that technological systems can be connected to one another.
		Explain that malfunctions of any part of a system may affect the function and quality of the system.
		Describe that trade-off is a decision process recognizing the need for careful compromises among competing factors.
		Explain that different technologies involve different sets of processes.
		Describe maintenance as a process of inspecting and servicing a product or system on a regular basis so that it continues to function properly, to extend life or upgrade its capability.
		Describe that controls are mechanisms or particular steps performed using information about the system that causes systems to change.
	3. Relationships among technologies and the connections between technology and other fields	Explain that technological systems often interact with one another.
		Explain that a product, system, or environment developed for one setting may be applied to another setting.
		Explain that knowledge from other fields has a direct effect on the development of technology.
Students will develop an understanding of Technology and Society.	Students will develop understanding of:	Students will be able to:
	4. Cultural, social, economic, and political effects of technology	Explain that the use of technology affects humans in various ways—safety, comfort, choices, and attitudes about technology's development and use.

113

		Explain that technology is neither good nor bad, but the decisions about the use of it can result in desirable or undesirable consequences.
		Explain that development and use of technology poses ethical questions.
		Explain that economic, political, and cultural issues are influenced by the development and use of technology.
	5. Effects of technology on the environment	Explain the management of waste produced by technological systems is a societal issue.
		Explain that technologies can be used to repair damage caused by natural disasters and break down wastes.
		Explain that the development and use of technologies put environmental and economic concerns in competition with one another.
	6. Role of society in the development and use of technology	Explain that throughout history new technologies have resulted from demands, values, and interests of individuals, businesses, industries, and societies.
		Explain that the use of inventions and innovations has led to changes in society and creation of new needs and wants.
		Explain that social and cultural priorities and values are reflected in the technological devices.
		Explain that meeting social expectations is the driving force behind the acceptance and use of products and systems.
	7. The influence of technology on history	Explain that many inventions and innovations have evolved by using a methodical process of tests and refinements.
		Explain the specialization of function has been at the head of many technological improvements.
		Explain that the design and construction of structures for service or convenience have evolved from the development of techniques for measurement, controlling systems, and understanding of spatial relationships.
		Explain that in the past, an invention or innovation was not usually developed with the knowledge of science.
Students will develop an understanding of Design	Students will develop an understanding of:	Students will be able to:
	8. The attributes of design	Describe design as a creative process that leads to useful products and systems.
		Explain there is no perfect design.
		Explain that the requirements for a design are made up of criteria and constraints.
	9. Engineering design	Explain that design involves a set of steps that can be performed in different sequences and repeated as needed.
		Describe brainstorming—a group problem-solving process in which each person presents their ideas in an open forum.
		Explain that modeling, testing, evaluating, and modifying are used to transform ideas into practical solutions.
	10. The role of troubleshooting, research and development, invention and innovation, and experimentation in problem solving	Describe troubleshooting as a way of identifying the cause of a malfunction in a technological system.
		Explain that invention is a process of turning ideas and imagination into devices and systems. Explain innovation is the process of modifying an existing product to improve it.

		Explain that some technological problems are best solved through science experimentations.
Students will develop abilities for a Technological World.	Students will be able to:	Students will be able to:
	11. Apply the design process	Apply a design process to solve a problem.
		Make two- and three-dimensional representations of the design solution.
		Test and evaluate the design related to pre-established criteria.
		Make a product or system and document the solution.
	12. Use and maintain technological products and systems	Use information provided to see and understand how things work.
		Use tools, materials, and machines safely to diagnose, adjust, and repair systems.
		Use computers and calculators in various applications.
		Operate and maintain systems in order to achieve a given purpose.
	13. Assess the impact of products and systems	Design and use instruments to gather data.
		Use data collected to analyze and interpret trends in order to identify the positive or negative effects of a technology.
		Identify trends and monitor potential consequences of technological development.
		Interpret and evaluate the accuracy of the information obtained, and determine if it is useful.
Students will develop an understanding of the Designed World.	Students will develop an understanding of and be able to select and use the following:	Students will be able to:
	14. Medical technologies	Explain advances in medical technologies are used to improve health care.
		Explain that sanitation processes used in the disposal of medical products help protect people from harmful organisms and disease and shape the ethics of medical safety.
		Explain that vaccines developed for immunizations require specialized technologies to support environments in which sufficient amounts of vaccines are produced.
		Describe that genetic engineering involves modifying the structure of DNA to produce novel genetic makeups.
	15. Agricultural and related biotechnologies	Explain that technological advances in agriculture affect the time and number of people required to produce food for large populations.
		Explain that a wide range of specialized equipment and practices are used to improve the production of food, fiber, fuel, and other products and in the care of animals.
		Describe that biotechnology applies the principles of biology to create products or processes.
		Explain that artificial ecosystems are human made environments that are designed to replicate a natural environment.
		Describe that the development of refrigeration, freezing, dehydration, preservation, and irradiation provide long-term storage of food and reduce the health risks of tainted food.

	16. Energy and power technologies	Explain that energy has the capacity to do work.
		Explain that energy can be used to do work using many processes.
		Explain that power is the rate at which energy is converted from one form to another, or transferred from one place to another, or the rate at which work is done.
		Describe that power systems are used to drive and provide propulsion to other products and systems.
		Explain that much of the energy used in our environment is not used efficiently.
	17. Information and communication technologies	Explain that information and communication allow information to be transferred from human to human, human to machine, and machine to human.
		Describe communication systems are made up of a source, encoder, transmitter, receiver, decoder, and destination.
		Describe that the design of a message is influenced by: intended audience, medium, purpose, and nature of the message.
		Explain the use of symbols, measurements, and drawings promotes clear communication by providing a common language to express ideas.
	18. Transportation technologies	Describe that transporting people and goods involves a combination of individuals or vehicles.
		Explain that transportation vehicles are made up of subsystems that must function together.
	19. Manufacturing technologies	Explain that manufacturing systems use mechanical processes that change the form of materials.
		Explain that manufactured goods can be durable or nondurable.
		Describe that the manufacturing process includes: designing, development, making, and servicing products and systems.
		Explain that chemical technologies are used to modify or alter chemical substances.
		Explain that materials must be located before they can be extracted from the earth.
		Explain that marketing involves informing the public about it as well as assisting in selling and distribution.
	20. Construction technologies	Explain that the selection of designs for structures is based on: building laws, codes, style, convenience, cost, climate, and function.
		Explain that structures rest on a foundation.
		Explain that some structures are temporary and some are permanent.
		Explain that buildings contain subsystems.

Assessment Answer Keys

Chapter One: Waste Management Issues (p. 15–16)

1. a   2. b   3. f   4. c
5. g   6. e   7. h   8. i
9. j   10. l   11. k   12. d
13. Environmental engineers try to solve problems related to air, water, and soil contamination.
14. Answers will vary.

Chapter 2: Solid Waste (p. 25–26)

1. d   2. a   3. e   4. c
5. f   6. h   7. i   8. b
9. g
10. Private haulers may not remove recyclable materials. They are just paid to haul, not to run a recycling operation.
11. Advantages – reduces the amount of wastes in the landfill, ashes are purified and can be used to cover wastes or to build roads, etc. Disadvantages – cost to build incinerators with scrubbers and other safety devices to keep from polluting the air
12. Composting advantages – reduces the amount of organic materials in the landfill, can be used as organic fertilizer
Disadvantages – need space to pile it, may smell, cannot put meat or meat products in your backyard
13. Answers will vary.
14. Recyclable materials can be remade into something else and reused. Non-recyclable materials cannot.

Chapter Three: Product Life Cycle (p. 41)

1. b   2. e   3. c   4. d
5. a
6. A life-cycle assessment examines all of the resources that are needed to create a product and the environmental impact of the product from its creation, through its use, up to its disposal. The environmental impact is the effect on the environment caused by humans or the technology that humans use.

7. Reduces resources needed, reduces pollution, reduces the amount of materials in landfills, etc.

8. A tree is cut down. Cutting down a tree requires a saw, some type of energy to power the saw, and some type of energy to pick up the pieces of the tree and load them onto some type of transportation to take the wood to the paper mill. Energy and resources are needed to transport the wood to the paper mill and unload it. When the tree arrives at the mill, the logs are chipped or ground into smaller pieces. Machines are needed to chop the wood into smaller pieces, and some type of energy and resources are needed to run the machines. The chipped wood is heated with water and other chemicals until the wood is soft and mushy. When the wood is soft and mushy, it is called pulp. Some energy and resources are needed to heat the water, make the chemicals needed to soften the wood, and make the containers that contain the pulp. The pulp is then put through machines with rollers to press the pulp into sheets. These roller machines require energy and resources to operate. Once the paper is made into sheets, it is allowed to dry. Once it is dry, the sheets are cut into smaller sheets, packaged, and transported to stores where the paper will be sold, which takes energy and resources. Consumers buy the paper for business or home use and transport the paper to where it will be used. Energy and resources are used when the consumer uses the paper. The paper is then discarded. Waste haulers pick up the discarded paper and recycle or put it into a landfill, which takes energy and resources. If the paper is recycled, the paper is sent back to a recycling facility where it is shredded and combined with water and other chemicals to create new pulp. The paper-making process starts over again.

Assessment Answer Keys (cont.)

Chapter Four: Composting (p. 55–56)

1. f   2. b   3. e   4. d
5. g   6. a   7. c   8. h
9. Aerobic microbes need a mixture of organic materials, water, and oxygen.
   Anaerobic microbes need a mixture of organic materials and water.
10. Compost needs a mixture of organic materials, water, and oxygen.
11. Microorganisms and larger organisms, along with heat, water, and oxygen (in aerobic composting), decompose organic material to produce carbon dioxide and energy. Also produced are water, methane, and hydrogen sulfide (depending on the process used). The final product left behind is humus.
12. yard trimmings, food scraps, wood waste, paper, animal manure, coffee grounds and filters, dryer and vacuum cleaner lint, cotton and wool rags, leaves, etc.

Chapter Five: The Five R's of Waste Management (p. 67–68)

1. h   2. i   3. k   4. j
5. l   6. m   7. n   8. a
9. b   10. c   11. d   12. e
13. o   14. f   15. g
16. Answers will vary.
17. Answers will vary.
18. Answers will vary.

Chapter Six: Packaging (p. 77–78)

1. Packaging protects products during distribution, storage, sale, and use. Packaging has various functions.
2. Ingredients, advertising, amount, nutritional information, warnings, etc.
3. For food allergies, special diets, safety, etc.
4. Plastic, wood, cardboard, aluminum, etc.
5. Pollution, some plastics do not disintegrate, they contain toxins, they are bulky, etc.
6. Answers will vary.

Chapter Seven: Landfill Construction (p. 92–93)

1. b   2. a   3. c   4. e
5. d   6. h   7. i   8. g
9. f   10. k
11. Answers will vary. 31% is paper; 13.2% yard wastes; 12.7% food; 12% plastic; 8.4 % metal; 7.9% rubber, leather, and textiles; 6.6% wood; 4.9% glass; and 3.3% other materials.
12. Answers will vary.
13. Answers should include how to control pollution, leachates, recycling, composting, gas-to-energy, etc.

Chapter Eight: STEM Design Challenge (p. 101)

Plans/models will vary.

References

Websites

About.Com: How School Lunch Packaging Waste Adds Up
http://environment.about.com/od/greenlivingdesign/a/school_lunch.htm

Alternative Energy News: Waste Energy
http://www.alternative-energy-news.info/technology/garbage-energy/

Amazing Kids
http://www.amazing-kids.org/kids3-00.htm

American Forest Foundation
http://www.affoundation.org/

American Forest & Paper Association
http://www.afandp.org/

Association of Post-Consumer Plastics Recyclers
http://www.plasticsrecycling.org/

Calculess: Environment Impact Analyzer
http://www.calculess.net/

The California Energy Commission: Landfill Gas Power Plants
http://www.energy.ca.gov/biomass/landfill_gas.htm

California Environmental Protection Agency Integrated Waste Board: Closing the Loop
http://www.calrecycle.ca.gov/Education/curriculum/CTL/TOC.htm

California Recycles: Home Composting
http://www.calrecycle.ca.gov/Organics/HomeCompost/

Coca-Cola: Sustainable Packaging
http://www.thecoca-colacompany.com/citizenship/plantbottle.html

Composting101.com
http://www.composting101.com/

Daily Dump: Composting
http://www.dailydump.org/composting

The Daily Green: What do Recycling Symbols on Plastics Mean?
http://www.thedailygreen.com/green-homes/latest/recycling-symbols-plastics-460321

3 Suspect Plastics to Avoid in Baby Bottles, Water Bottles, More
http://www.thedailygreen.com/green-homes/eco-friendly/plastic-bottles-toxins-water-bottles-460410

Department of Ecology: State of Washington: A Way with Waste Resources
http://www.ecy.wa.gov/programs/air/aawwaste/awwresources.html

Earth 911: Composting in the City
http://earth911.com/news/2010/08/30/composting-in-the-city/

Earth 911: The Biology of Composting
http://earth911.com/news/2007/04/02/the-biology-of-composting/

Earth Odyssey, LLC: Recycling Symbols
http://earthodyssey.com/symbols.html

Earth Pack
http://www.earthpack.com/

Education World: How Long Does Trash Last?
http://www.educationworld.com/a_lesson/03/lp308-04.shtml

Energy Recovery Council: Waste to Energy
http://www.wte.org

Engineering is Elementary: Engineering and Technology Lessons for Children
http://www.mos.org/EiE

Engineer Girl
http://www.engineergirl.org/

Engineering Challenges
http://www.engineeringchallenges.org/

Engineering K-12
http://egfi-k12.org/

Engineering, Science, and Mathematics Careers
http://www.khake.com/page53.html

Engineer Your Life
http://www.engineeryourlife.org/

Environmental Literacy Council: Landfills
http://www.enviroliteracy.org/article.php/63.html

Environmental Protection Agency (EPA)
www.epa.gov/

Composting
http://www.epa.gov/epawaste/conserve/rrr/
composting/index.htm

Compost and Fertilizer Made From Recovered Organic Materials
http://www.epa.gov/epawaste/conserve/tools/
cpg/products/compost.htm

Energy Projects and Candidate Landfills
http://www.epa.gov/lmop/projects-candidates/
index.html

Guide for Industrial Waste Management
http://www.epa.gov/epawaste/nonhaz/
industrial/guide/index.htm

Inventory of Greenhouse Gas Emissions and Sinks: 1990 – 2008
http://www.epa.gov/climatechange/emissions/
usinventoryreport.html

Landfill Methane Outreach Program
http://www.epa.gov/lmop/index.html

Landfill Reclamation
http://www.epa.gov/osw/nonhaz/
municipal/landfill/land-rcl.pdf

Landfills
http://www.epa.gov/epawaste/nonhaz/
municipal/landfill.htm

Non-Hazardous Wastes
http://www.epa.gov/epawaste/basic-solid.htm

Innovative Packaging
http://blog.epa.gov/blog/2010/03/25/
innovative-packaging/

Pesticides: Topical & Chemical Fact Sheets
http://www.epa.gov/opp00001/factsheets/
foodfyi.htm

Packaging
http://www.epa.gov/wastes/partnerships/
stewardship/products/packaging.htm

Paper Recycling: Frequent Questions
http://www.epa.gov/osw/conserve/
materials/paper/faqs.htm#

Planet Protectors Club for Kids
http://www.epa.gov/epawaste/education/kids/
planetprotectors/index.htm

The Quest for Less
http://www.epa.gov/wastes/education/quest/
pdfs/qfl_complete.pdf

Reduce, Reuse, Recycle
http://www.epa.gov/epawaste/conserve/rrr/
index.htm

Reducing and Recycling
http://www.epa.gov/epawaste/conserve/
materials/organics/reduce.htm

Solid Waste Management and Greenhouse Gases: A Life-Cycle Assessment of Emissions and Sinks
http://epa.gov/climatechange/wycd/waste/
downloads/fullreport.pdf

Transfer Stations For Non-Hazardous Waste
http://www.epa.gov/epawaste/nonhaz/
municipal/transfer.htm

Waste Reduction Through Conservation
http://www.epa.gov/epawaste/conserve/rrr/
reduce.htm

Wastes
www.epa.gov/epawaste/

Waste Wise
http://www.epa.gov/wastes/partnerships/
wastewise/

Florida's Online Composting Center: Virtual Compost Pile
http://www.compostinfo.com/cn/Default.htm

Food and Drug Administration
http://www.fda.gov/

Recycled Plastics in Food Packaging
http://www.fda.gov/food/
foodingredientspackaging/
foodcontactsubstancesfcs/ucm093435.htm

Food Ingredients and Packaging Terms
http://www.fda.gov/Food/
FoodIngredientsPackaging/ucm064228.htm

Fun Science Gallery: Making and Recycling Paper at Home
http://www.funsci.com/fun3_en/paper/paper.htm

Girl Scouts: Girls Go Tech
http://www.girlsgotech.org/engineer.html

Greatest Engineering Achievements of the 20th Century
http://www.greatachievements.org/

How Stuff Works Express
http://express.howstuffworks.com/

> **How Composting Works**
> http://www.howstuffworks.com/composting.htm/

> **How Landfills Work**
> http://www.howstuffworks.com/
> environmental/green-science.landfill.htm/

How to Compost
http://www.howtocompost.org/info/info_
composting.asp

Inventions and Technology
http://kids.nypl.org/science/inventions.cfm

Inventions, Inventors, and You
http://www.ih.k12.oh.us/MSHERRMANN/Invent2.htm

Inventors and Inventions
http://edtech.kennesaw.edu/web/inventor.html

Kids Gardening: Making Paper
http://www.kidsgardening.com/growingideas/
projects/nov02/pg1.html

Kid Inventions: Inventions for School
http://inventors.about.com/od/kidinventions/ss/
Young_Inventors.htm

Kids Konnect: Inventors and Inventions
http://www.kidskonnect.com/subject-index/
15-science/86-inventors-a-inventions.html

Kids Recycling Zone
http://www.kidsrecyclingzone.com/

Lemelson Center for the Study of Invention and Innovation
http://invention.smithsonian.org/resources/sites_
teachers.aspx

Making Paper from Plants
http://www.missioncreekpress.com/plants.htm

National Academy of Engineers
http://www.nae.edu

National Center for Technological Literacy: Museum of Science, Boston
http://www.nctl.org/

> **Our Nation's Challenge**
> http://www.nctl.org/our_nations_challenge.php

National Museum of Education: Invention
http://nmoe.org/students/index.htm

National Solid Waste Management Association (NSWMA)
http://www.environmentalistseveryday.org/

> **Electronic Wastes**
> http://www.environmentalistseveryday.org/
> issues-solid-waste-technologies-regulations/
> e-waste-disposal-electronics-products-computer-
> recycling/index.php

> **History of Solid Waste Management**
> http://www.environmentalistseveryday.org/
> publications-solid-waste-industry-research/
> information/history-of-solid-waste-managment/
> index.php

> **Landfills**
> http://www.environmentalistseveryday.org/
> issues-solid-waste-technologies-regulations/
> landfills-garbage-disposal/index.php

> **Recycling**
> http://www.environmentalistseveryday.org/
> issues-solid-waste-technologies-regulations/
> recycling-waste/index.php

> **Source Reduction**
> http://www.environmentalistseveryday.org/
> issues-solid-waste-technologies-regulations/
> source-reduction-solid-waste/index.php

Natural Resources Conservation Service
http://www.nrcs.usda.gov/feature/backyard/
Compost.html

New York Public Library On-Lion: Inventions Changed Our World
http://teacher.scholastic.com/lessonrepro/
lessonplans/theme/inventions.htm

Package Design Magazine
http://www.packagedesignmag.com/

Packaging Law
http://www.packaginglaw.com/

Packaging Science
http://www.ist.rit.edu/~pscidrupal/

Paperboard Packaging
http://www.paperboardpackaging.org/

Paper University
http://www.tappi.org/paperu/welcome.htm

Pew Center on Global Climate Change: Pattonville High School Landfill Gas Recovery Project
http://www.pewclimate.org/node/4112

Pioneer Thinking: Making Paper
http://www.pioneerthinking.com/makingpaper.html

The Plastics Web
http://www.ides.com/resources/plastic-recycling-codes.asp

Power Scorecard: Electricity From Landfill Gas
http://powerscorecard.org/tech_detail.cfm?resource_id=5

Project Learning Tree
http://www.plt.org/

Recology
http://recology.com/

> **Residential Compost Collection Program**
> http://sunsetscavenger.com/residentialCompost.htm

Recycle Plastic Containers
http://www.sks-bottle.com/Recycle_Plastic.html

The Responsible Package
http://theresponsiblepackage.com/

Rotten Truth About Garbage
http://www.astc.org/exhibitions/rotten/rthome.htm/

San Francisco's Department of the Environment
http://www.sfenvironment.org/

Think Quest: Making Paper from Recycled Paper
http://library.thinkquest.org/4054/recyc/pap.mak/papermaking.1.html

The University of Florida IFAS Extension: Consumer Choices Can Reduce Packaging Waste
http://edis.ifas.ufl.edu/ae226

University of New Hampshire: Cogeneration Plant & Landfill Gas Pipeline
http://www.sustainableunh.unh.edu/climate_ed/cogen_landfillgas.html

Use Less Stuff
http://www.use-less-stuff.com/index.htm

> **An Ounce of Prevention**
> http://www.use-less-stuff.com/An-Ounce-of-Prevention.pdf

VegWeb.com: Introduction to Composting
http://www.vegweb.com/composting/

Weyerhaeuser: Growing Ideas
http://www.growingideas.com/#/WhatCanATreeBe/

Wisconsin Paper Council
http://www.wipapercouncil.org/

> **The Invention of Paper**
> http://www.wipapercouncil.org/invention.htm

> **Paper Making Process**
> http://www.wipapercouncil.org/process.htm

> **Paper in Wisconsin: Make Paper**
> http://www.wipapercouncil.org/makepaper.htm

> **Paper in Wisconsin: Fun Facts**
> http://www.wipapercouncil.org/funfacts.htm

WasteAge: Crystalline Vision
http://www.wasteage.com/Landfill_Management/crystalline_vision_lmop_lfgte/

> **Profiles in Garbage**
> http://wasteage.com/waste-facts/

Waste Management: Think Green
http://www.thinkgreen.com/recycle-what-detail?sec=plastics&prod=plastic-recycling-code

Waste Online: Packaging Recycling Information Sheet
http://www.wasteonline.org.uk/resources/InformationSheets/Packaging.htm

World Health Organization: Waste Management
http://www.wpro.who.int/health_topics/waste_management/

Books

Appelhof, Mary. *Worms Eat My Garbage: How to Set Up and Maintain a Worm Composting System.* Kalamazoo, MI: Flower Press. 1997.

Campbell, Stu. *Let it Rot!: The Gardener's Guide to Composting.* North Adams, MA: Storey Publishers, LLC. 1998.

Center for Mathematics, Science, and Technology Education. *Integrated Mathematics, Science, and Technology: Waste Management.* Peoria, IL: Glencoe McGraw-Hill. 1999.

Gershuny, Grace, and Deborah L. Martin, eds. *The Rodale Book of Composting: Easy Methods for Every Gardener.* Emmaus, PA: Rodale Books. 1992.

Illinois Department of Commerce. *4R's: Recycling Lessons and Projects: An Illinois School Teacher's Guide.* Springfield, IL: Illinois Department of Commerce and Economic Opportunity. 2009.

Winter, Jonah. *Here Comes the Garbage Barge!* New York: Schwartz & Wade. 2010.